CONSERVATORIES
AND GARDEN ROOMS

CONSERVATORIES
AND GARDEN ROOMS

Alexander Bartholomew
Jill Blake
Brent Elliott
Mike Lawrence
Katherine Panchyk
Denys de Saulles
Tom Wellsted

General Editor: Jasmine Taylor

Macdonald

A Macdonald Book

© The Rainbird Publishing Group Ltd

First published in Great Britain in 1985
by Macdonald & Co (Publishers) Ltd
London & Sydney

A member of BPCC plc

British Library Cataloguing in Publication Data

Conservatories and garden rooms.
  1. Garden Rooms
  I. Bartholomew, Alexander
  643'.55   SB419

  ISBN 0-356-10495-8

Typeset by Bookworm Typesetting Ltd, Manchester, England
Illustrations originated by Bridge Graphics Ltd, Hull, England
Printed and bound by Artes Gráficas Toledo, S.A. Spain

This book was designed and produced by
The Rainbird Publishing Group Ltd
`40 Park Street, London W1Y 4DE

Picture researcher: Janice Lacock
Illustrator: Trevor Lawrence
Indexer: Vicky Robinson

Macdonald & Co (Publishers) Ltd
Maxwell House
74 Worship Street
London EC2A 2EN
D. L. TO: 1833 -1984

Contents

Introduction

There has been a significant revival in recent years of what was traditionally known, especially in the 19th century, as the conservatory. The romantic and nostalgic associations this term conjures up are, however, somewhat misleading in the context of the present day. With advances in technology and materials, it is fair to say that garden rooms, attached greenhouses and other glasshouse extensions have created totally new living experiences, going far beyond the use to which the original conservatory was once put. The growing trend towards a glasshouse extension is based, in large part, on traditional principles of conservatory design – a thin-framed building incorporating a large surface area of glass. Unlike many other modern forms of building extension, the glasshouse is able to blend in with and conform to the different styles of the home or city apartment to which it is attached. It is this versatility – and, of course, the benefits of flowering plants – that gives it such an advantage over other room designs. Because there is always some confusion between such terms as greenhouse and conservatory the terms, as used in this book, are interchangeable. Throughout we are speaking of the contemporary attached glass-enclosed room.

In the past, the value of a glasshouse extension was certainly limited, yet the advances made in building techniques have now enabled this type of structure to be used for a whole range of domestic activities. A fully glazed home extension has been developed that is technically efficient, extremely flexible in terms of application, and in the majority of cases visually acceptable – even in its standard pre-fabricated form.

It is little wonder, therefore, that with these qualities – and the economy of construction afforded by new materials and building techniques – the 'new conservatory' is today enjoying a revival as a practical and efficient type of home extension.

The need to grow

With the increasing costs of moving – and the problems of finding the right kind of property in the right location – many families are looking at alternative solutions to the difficulties faced by growing households or changed life-styles.

There is probably no other type of domestic construction that can take better advantage of technology and materials than factory-made, standardized components for greenhouses that are easily assembled on the site. The recent resurgence in the popularity of the glass conservatory as an additional room, in a market that has previously been dominated by brick and mortar

The traditional Victorian conservatory, with its black-and-white tiled floor and jungle of plants, was one way of the owners proclaiming their affluence. However, the escalating cost of the necessary labour for servicing and maintenance in those days was certainly one reason for the conservatory's demise.

or wood-frame types of building, is partly due to the reduced cost of manufacture and ease of assembly. Apart from the work involved in preparing the foundations and a suitable sub-structure, which is relatively simple and inexpensive, a modern conservatory – whether it has an aluminium or timber frame -- can be quickly assembled on site from components or even complete walls already prepared and made up in the factory. In other words, what is often the most expensive and certainly most labour-intensive part of the job – the on-site work – is kept to the minimum.

Another major advantage lies in the fact that a conservatory can be put up at virtually any time throughout the year, since its construction is not dependent on suitable weather conditions – except in extreme cold. Apart from the foundations, the assembly work is 'dry'. This means that, since the main components are fitted together with simple mechanical fixings, once the prefabricated structure is delivered the installation can be carried out even in wet or frosty conditions.

To make a fully-glazed room such as a conservatory habitable all through the year, it is essential to overcome the basic problems inherent in traditional designs. These include condensation, heat gain and loss and all-round insulation. Condensation and heat loss can be reduced to a tolerable level by improving the insulation. In the case of a conservatory, this means double or even triple glazing on the walls and roof. Even this, however, is not always enough, and techniques are now available which improve the insulation properties of factory-sealed glazed units even further.

One method involves filling the gap between the two panes of glass that make up the sealed unit with argon, a gas that reduces the transmittance of heat from the warmer inner pane to the colder outer pane. There are also types of 'energy' glass with special coatings that reflect heat back into the room. When incorporated in a double-glazed sealed unit, these types of glass can perform better than standard triple-glazed systems. Their effectiveness can be measured by the fact that the heat loss through 'energy' glass in a double-glazed sealed unit can be as much as two-thirds less than that through a single pane of standard glass.

Sophisticated glazing techniques have also been developed to cope with the equally significant problem of increases in heat in fully glazed rooms. The transmittance of solar heat through a glass roof or wall can be limited or reduced either by reflection or by the glass itself absorbing the heat. Solar-control glass that

Today's conservatory tends to be a fully integrated part of the home. Here a contemporary drawing room has been extended into a plant-filled glass extension, which attractively and economically enlarges the living area.

reflects heat is generally the most effective – but also the most expensive. Another disadvantage is that because it can have a mirror-like appearance on the outside, it may look unsuitable in certain locations. Other tinted types of glass, which absorb heat and are cheaper may suit the image of the traditional conservatory better, although they are slightly less efficient. They are commonly available in grey or bronze tints of varying intensity. Further, various types of shades are available for installation both inside and outside the greenhouse or conservatory.

The glass revolution

The developments in manufacture and treatment of glass, with the advances made in the associated framing and sealing systems, have brought about a fundamental revolution in architectural design at many levels. For literally thousands of years architects have struggled within the resources available to them first to enclose space and then to light it. The traditional methods of building design reflect their efforts to achieve a compromise between enclosed space and light.

Fortunately today those advances in material technology have allowed designers far greater scope than ever before. Now they can design buildings in which a wall can be a window and a window can be a wall. Thus, current building technology has brought the attributes of the conservatory within reach of residential builders and home and apartment owners who desire glass rooms that afford flexibility and attractive space at reasonable cost.

Choosing and Siting

There are various reasons for choosing a conservatory or greenhouse as opposed to other types of extension. Having decided that more space must be created and having considered the many alternatives, your choice will have been made on the basis of what the conservatory can offer in terms of appearance, design, versatility and cost that the other types of extension cannot afford.

Making it work

Whatever the initial reason for deciding on a conservatory, its usefulness will to a large extent depend on its relationship to adjoining rooms and their functions. The most obvious reasons for extending a particular room is because space for the activity carried out in it is restricted by its size.

An extension to the kitchen, for example, can provide a breakfast or dining room. An extension to the living room can create a more formal dining room or less formal living room or nursery. Sometimes it is possible to link rooms by means of a garden room conservatory, making that space accessible from different rooms that previously had no relationship or direct link. In this case it is easy to undervalue the additional new space, since the effects it can have on the existing adjoining rooms can be quite dramatic.

Anyone considering a conservatory or similar glass-enclosed extension should always regard it as a method of changing or improving the design of the rest of the house. If it is thought of as a separate, albeit useful, addition, its value will easily be under-estimated and it could, with lack of careful planning, actually detract from the quality and efficiency of the existing space. However practical and attractive the conservatory may appear in itself, its effect on an adjoining room could be disastrous if its role is reduced to that of a passage – and becomes, therefore, difficult to furnish and use in its own right.

To illustrate clearly the questions that must be answered before finally deciding on a conservatory as the ideal choice for a room extension, it is important to establish the projected function of the new area and hence the type of structure which is best suited to that function.

The right exposure

Any predominantly or fully-glazed room will give its occupants a feeling of being exposed. Although not in itself an undesirable sensation – and one that needs to appeal if a conservatory is the final choice – it obviously excludes certain, more private, functions, such as bathing or sleeping. However, this feature should be of positive value in providing more light for the adjoining room than could be offered from the more traditional type of home extension.

Normally a single room extension would be accessible through a doorway created in an existing window opening. Even if this is not the case, it is still more than likely that the new structure will cover or block out existing windows and therefore rob adjoining rooms of daylight. In this situation an extension with a glazed roof has obvious advantages, since its transparency interferes far less with the transmission of natural light into the existing rooms.

It is worth remembering that the glass roof is much more important that the glazed walls in maintaining a sufficent amount of light for adjoining rooms. The steeper the angle of natural light permitted by a glass roof, the less the quality of light in the linking

When choosing a conservatory it is important to consider its relationship to existing adjoining rooms and their functions. The conservatory below provides a self-contained living/dining area, plus a covered walkway to an outbuilding. The conservatory on the right, however, makes no attempt to be self-contained – it has increased the original floor space to incorporate a music and work area which is very much a part of the original room.

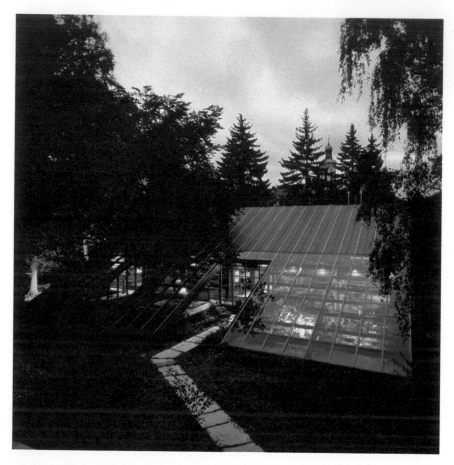

This triangular glasshouse was built on conservatory principles. With such an enormous expanse of glass, heating would be difficult but solar panels in the roof help solve the problem.

room will be affected. A bright, busy room can easily be turned into a gloomy, unused one, thus negating the value of the additional space which merely becomes a replacement.

From a lighting point of view, therefore, it is obvious that for itself and the rooms it adjoins, the conservatory has a distinct advantage over the more usual brick-built extensions.

Controlling the internal environment

While a glass structure has obvious advantages over the more solidly built extensions, heating can prove a disadvantage. So, despite the technical improvements being made in the insulation qualities of standard glazing systems, with a conservatory wanted for living in it is usually essential to install some sort of insulated glazing system.

Although double-glazed or otherwise insulated conservatories are relatively costly to heat in particularly cold weather, for much of the year the heat they take in from the outside can be used to heat other parts of the house or the water – by means of solar panels.

The full potential of the conservatory as a means of collecting solar energy is not commonly realized. But the choice of a conservatory as an extension to the existing building will certainly justify the costs involved in ducting and altering existing services in the house to utilize this form of free energy. There are, in fact, some new housing developments in which this practical feature has been recognized by designing-in a conservatory at the planning stage. So it now seems likely that this type of structure will, in some form or other, become a standard component of new, energy-efficient housing, especially in locations where good sunlight is plentiful.

Some relatively simple air-circulating devices are available for fitting into existing buildings and new conservatories. There is, for example, an electric fan that, when installed in the wall between the conservatory and the house, preferably near the ceiling, will drive air from the warmer to the cooler space. This means that on a bright sunny day it will extract hot air from the conservatory and blow it into the house, while, on a cold night, it will reverse this action and blow warm air from the house into the conservatory.

The greatest environmental control problem comes from over-heating. The degree of this problem will depend on where the conservatory is sited. For example, on a south-facing wall, even in mild sunshine, conditions can become insufferable if the right controls are not provided.

There are three ways of maintaining a normal temperature inside a conservatory – by shading, reflection and ventilation.

Shading systems in the form of blinds or louvres are most effective when used outside the conservatory. Special tinted glass will effectively shade the inside and absorb heat. Solar heat can be reflected most successfully using special solar control glass that has a high reflective coating. This type of glass tends to be more expensive than the tinted one, but its performance in reducing the overall heat transmittance is better and it does not overheat, which can be a problem with tinted glass. The third method of reducing the heat level in the conservatory, ventilation, can be achieved by natural convection – rising hot air is dispelled through vents situated in the roof, or by mechanical extraction.

Because the various systems for controlling temperature inside the conservatory can be elaborate and costly, it is important to consider at an early stage whether an alternative location could be used to avoid the problem.

Siting it right

Bearing in mind the changing strength of the sun during the day, the ideal situations to consider when siting a conservatory or greenhouse are those where the glass roof faces either east or west. While allowing a degree of sunshine, which is of course desirable, in these situations the sun is less intense in the early morning or evening.

As well as considering the amount of potential sunshine falling on the conservatory, an equally relevant point to remember is the time of day the room is most likely to be in use. The conservatory that will be used at breakfast time, for example, should make the most of the early morning sun, while one that is to be used primarily in the evening, possibly as a dining room, should catch the rays of the setting sun.

Of course, there are also aesthetic considerations to take into account before deciding on the site. Although in some respects these are not as crucial as the practical considerations of which rooms need to be extended and where the sunshine is coming from, they are relevant to the overall enjoyment of the new room if an option on siting is still available.

A small conservatory doubles as an entrance hall and a plant room. Constant draughts created by the opening and closing of the door, however, will limit the choice of plants.

In dull northern latitudes (1) the long axis of a conservatory should be orientated east-west to make full use of what sun there is. In more southerly and sunny coastal regions (2), however, its long axis should be northeast-southwest which will lessen the overheating effect from midday onwards.

Whether you choose a conservatory or other type of extension, you must always remember that it is an addition to a previously designed, compact and self-contained building and a potential intrusion into an established garden.

This aspect of the conservatory's location reflects the traditional concept of a glasshouse as a link between house and garden. If a choice of site is available, careful thought should be given to the view from the conservatory – particularly, for example, if the garden beyond contains a specially attractive feature or there is a panorama beyond its boundary.

It is the relationship with the garden that is all too easily overlooked, since the extension is frequently relegated to its position as an afterthought because other aspects of the home and its environment appear more pressing. Special features that can be combined with this type of extension include a terrace, patio or space for barbecue. It is surprising how much these elements help to soften the often sharp distinction between house and garden – the man-made environment and the more natural one.

The opportunity provided by the modern conservatory to smooth out this division, by accommodating domestic functions and at the same time offering a link with the natural world outside, should not be missed, as it could so easily be by careless planning and poor siting.

The attractions of a glass building are obvious. Because of its transparency, it enables the garden to be seen from the house and provides a natural link between the house and garden. This is in contrast to other forms of extension, whose effect is often to intrude on this natural area.

Keeping a clear head

While a structure with a glass roof has many advantages, the roof does present two problems that may well limit the choice or design of the extension – those of height and pitch. For a glass roof to be self-cleaning, it requires a minimum pitch of about 25 degrees. Although current glazing systems enable the roof to remain waterproof at extremely low pitches, there is more likelihood of a build-up of dirt and rubbish on the glass. This will not only look unsightly from both inside and outside, but will also defeat the object of having a glass roof to let in light.

Problems which may arise due to the desired pitch of the conservatory roof can, however, be overcome. Obvious examples of these include extending from a single-storey building or one that has low first-floor windows. In either case, it may be possible to pitch the glass roof from a point at eaves level, thus achieving the required slope. Equally the conservatory roof may slope down on all sides and its peak or ridge could be higher than the building it adjoins.

With this type of design, it would be necessary to install a box or valley gutter where the glass roof adjoins the existing structure in order to take the rainwater. Provided that this guttering is properly fitted and maintained, there should be no problems.

The significant point to bear in mind is that the height of the glass extension's roof is very much part of the building's character and that this feature is particularly noticeable when people walk into the extension from the adjoining room with its lower ceiling. Also, the height of the roof plays an important part in the ventilation of the extension by increasing the effectiveness of convection, for aiding heat control.

The height of the conservatory or garden room will be determined to a certain extent by its proposed function. But its suitability as an addition to an existing building must be considered. The glass extension to the right has been designed to fit neatly beneath the sloping roof, while the one on the left makes full use of the available height by reaching to the top of the main house to give an enormous glassed-in area.

Choosing the right design

Having looked at the problems of siting and control of its internal environment, the next consideration must be the type and design of the glasshouse. There are several different approaches: you can design the extension yourself, seeking technical advice from a builder and letting him construct it; you can engage the services of a suitably qualified architect, telling him what you have in mind and, after accepting his proposals, ask him to employ a builder and supervise the construction.

The right conservatory in the right place – these eight colour illustrations are just a few examples of the large range now available. Ranging from a tiny prism-like structure to fit a small patio through lean-to's to all-round-the-house glass constructions, they give an idea of the versatility of these attractive glass extensions.

Another option is to shop around among the specialist manufacturers of such buildings and select the type that best suits your needs and situation, checking of course on the competitiveness of the quotations you receive. In addition, there are consultants who will help you to choose by explaining what is available on the market and advising on the most suitable, keeping in mind your budget and basic requirements. These people work either on a commission basis with the manufacturers or for a fee that would be charged to you.

Before you commit yourself to designing your own conserva-

Yet another variation on the theme – a pretty, wooden-framed structure to fit on to a balcony or rooftop.

tory, it is worth considering that the only likely satisfaction you will gain from the exercise is that you have your own, personal structure. Unless you also build it, the exercise will prove relatively expensive and, more importantly, there is real danger of design and construction faults because of your inexperience.

Probably the most common fault when one chooses a local builder is that he is unfamiliar with glasshouse construction and compounds his inexperience by ignoring the specialist who could advise on appropriate roof-glazing systems. As a result such a builder often seals the glass with putty alone or beds the glass in putty under a timber cover strip. In both cases – or even if he uses a special proprietary self-adhesive to cover flashings – the maximum waterproof life achieved is only likely to be of a few years' duration.

Of course, building or designing yourself can be great fun (some say) and prove sufficiently inexpensive if you are prepared to tolerate a certain number of faults in the design or workmanship. That is for you to decide. Although it would cost more to have an architect hire a builder, a good one will more than justify his fee by not only providing professional expertise in terms of the design but also by choosing the right builder for the job and supervising the work. This approach will almost certainly be necessary where an awkward site is chosen, or when there is a difficult fit to the existing building. If you use an architect, make sure you choose one who has experience in glasshouse construction. The same applies to the builder if you supervise the work. You will also need to satisfy yourself that the people you choose are able to exploit all aspects of planning to the best advantage in achieving the ideal relationship with the existing building and in providing a space that properly serves all the purposes to which it is to be put.

The right people for the job

When people are having domestic building done they often adopt a popular – but particularly unfortunate – attitude towards architects that is neither fair on the profession nor of value to the client. All too often the architect is used to do the dirty work, by acting as a go-between, whether it is chasing the local authority for the necessary approvals or beating down the builder's prices both before and during the work. Rarely is he given sufficient opportunity to exercise his talents and reveal his imagination – in short to design. Almost inevitably, therefore, he is blamed for any problems that arise, particularly in the relationship between the client and the builder – whether involving workmanship, timing or cost.

It is crucial to the ultimate success of the work to choose the right profession for the job to be done and, more particularly, the right person within that profession or trade. This, of course, is easier said than done. But the safest method, if you do not already have people whom you know and trust, is to find examples of the type and style of conservatory or greenhouse you like and to contact those people responsible for all aspects of the work as well as others who have had similar work done for them. It's always wise to check references before selecting architects or builders and then to inspire each to do the best job possible. This rarely happens if you limit their creativity, are unclear about the precise result desired and the budget, or if you hound them to death.

Keeping up appearances

In considering the type and style of conservatory that will best suit your requirements, it is vital to ensure that the extension

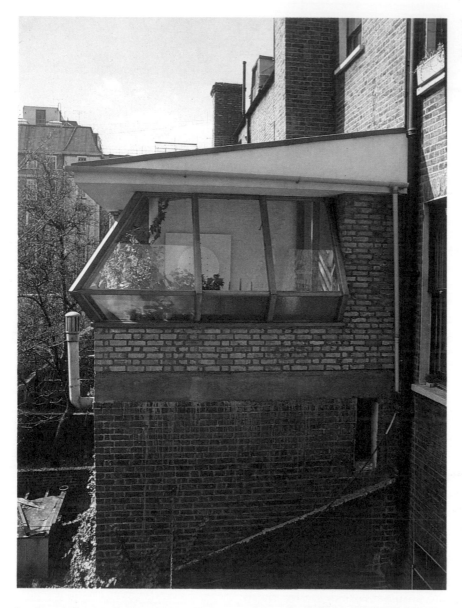

The angled windows and wedge-like roof of this architect-designed extension combine to make a pleasing modern living area.

looks right in the context of the existing building. It is obviously an expensive operation to try to match materials and craftsmanship when extending on to an older, traditional building in an attempt to maintain a rigidly exact style. Despite the fact that a greenhouse or conservatory obviously has been added on, it can be done in such a way that it is totally acceptable from a visual and aesthetic point of view. Depending on the style of the building, there is still choice to suit it within the types of conservatory available. Be certain to have the design of the glass extension, especially its slender lines, type of glass, and possibly

24

arch-topped windows, match the proportions of the existing building.

A conservatory with glass walls subdivided by glazing bars into small rectangular panes would, for example, suit buildings constructed when large panes of glass were not available. In contrast, a conservatory with large uninterrupted areas of glass held in place with either stained timber or anodized aluminium framing would be ideal as an extension to more modern houses.

These examples are, of course, simplifications and careful planning of the design is needed to ensure that the style suits a particular building. What needs to be achieved is a comfortable blend of design and materials to enhance both the new and old structures and to create an acceptable degree of harmony.

One aspect of any extension work that is all too often ignored is the effect it has on the outdoor area around the original building. The inevitable result of any addition to the house is the creation of new enclosed spaces, where previously the space outside the building was open. For example, a square garden behind a rectangular house is immediately subdivided and redefined. So a conservatory that protrudes from a flat back of a house will create special places either side of it which will then have, for example, light and wind conditions quite different from the previous ones.

Shopping around

If you are confident that you have made the correct choice by deciding on a conservatory and you know the type you want and where you want to position it, and have decided not to build it yourself or hire an architect, then the next stage is to shop around those firms specializing in prefabricated conservatories, which may have exactly the type you are looking for. Companies and their products vary and you will have to study carefully each catalogue and visit a number of displays to get the style, quality and aesthetics you are after at a price you can afford.

There are certain obvious points to watch for. For example, if you want the conservatory for an extension that is to be used all the year round, you need to check on the double glazing and draught seals in doors and windows. In short, it needs to have quality and permanence which matches that of the existing building. Unless you require the conservatory for house plants alone or summer use only, you should avoid single glazing. Apart from the heat loss through such glass, condensation could be a problem if the structure is not properly ventilated.

You must pay close attention to various technical aspects of conservatory construction for, despite what may be an overall attractive appearance, the one you buy could turn out to be an expensive, unusable ornament. To help you with your search, you should therefore make a list of the minimum standards and facilities you will need from your glass extension. This will not only save you a certain amount of time, but it will also give you ammunition with which to counteract the inevitable sales talk. The list should include such things as insulation, draught exclusion, wall and roof ventilation, and potential condensation problems, provision for blind and shading systems, maintenance (especially above roof glass) and security.

It is likely that from the range of glass extensions available only a few will satisfy all your requirements. From this small number you will be in a position to make a final choice based on aesthetic considerations: appearance, any special features, and compatibility with the existing building.

It is difficult to advise on this aspect of choice, but any decision you make will inevitably be a personal one, coloured by your own attitudes and experiences. Fortunately, your instinct will tell you when you have made the right choice. If you have a nagging doubt about some aspect of a particular type or design, do not despair – and do not settle for something that is only nearly right. Any compromise made at this stage will be a continual source of irritation later on.

Do not be in too much of a hurry to make your choice. Keep looking and bear in mind if that you can identify minor shortcomings in a design that you basically like, you may be able to persuade the manufacturer to carry out the necessary alterations to give you what you need. Some specialist firms are more rigid than others and may not be able to vary their standard range without involving themselves – and therefore the buyer – in extra cost. Most types of conservatory advertised are based, however, on modular systems which enable the manufacturer to offer a selection of components in different combinations of design.

You may find you need an exact size or shape of conservatory to fit an existing base or to suit a precisely defined area. In this case, it is often possible to use a majority of components from a standard system and include the necessary one-off but matching components to achieve the required result. Smaller companies – and those that also handle the installation work – may well be in a position to design, manufacture and fit these special components. If you are fortunate, this additional work may be done at no extra cost, if the company is prepared to regard the modification as essential in achieving the sale against less flexible opposition.

27

Getting what you want

In assessing the suitability of a particular product – or, for that matter, the manufacturer – it is important to establish how well they can satisfy your brief and exactly what is included in their quoted price. If there are to be any extras, you must know before you order. Some firms, for example, may charge extra for the initial site visit and preliminary discussions. Some will be prepared to handle any applications and subsequent negotiations with local councils or other relevant authorities, whose permission may have to be sought before any work can commence. Others will expect you to cope with these items yourself or to employ a surveyor to do so.

There will be the preparatory work of constructing the foundations and possibly providing for drainage, which specialist manufacturers may not handle themselves. If they do not, you can, however, expect them to supply the necessary drawings and specifications for a builder to follow. Some firms will recommend 'approved' builders with whom they have worked in the past. This can be a wise choice, since they should have first-hand experience of any peculiarities in that particular type of building and know how to cope with them.

To sum up: when you go to a specialist, you must know not only what you are buying from them but also the cost of any additional services or materials you will need in order to complete the project.

Provided you can find the right type of conservatory on the market, even if this involves having minor modifications made, you will find that using a specialist manufacturer should prove the best value in terms of quality and cost.

The conservatory market is now booming and there are many new ideas and designs on the way. As the options grow, your choice will become more difficult but at least you will have a better chance of finding the conservatory you always dreamed of.

A traditional role

In this chapter, attention has been concentrated on the new role that the glass or conservatory-style building can have as a permanent, habitable house or apartment extension. There is still, nonetheless, a considerable interest in this type of building serving its traditional role as a summer room, plant room or perhaps a rather up-market attached – and so comfortably accessible – greenhouse. As such, or to house similar activities,

An unusual but perfectly viable use for a glass extension – a bathroom. If the site is secluded little is needed in the way of 'window dressing', but in a more open situation, roller blinds or carefully positioned plants will provide the required degree of privacy.

the conservatory is usually a product of the leisure or garden-building industry.

The well-established and technically-advanced manufacture and marketing of these wood or aluminium-framed structures now reflects the new opportunity presented by the rebirth of the conservatory. With long experience in the greenhouse and garden building market, companies now offer a range of refined models to meet the new requirements more closely associated with domestic activities.

There are many suitable glass buildings on the market – and at competitive prices. Provided their limited application – as conservatories in the traditional sense – is appreciated, you will have no trouble finding the right type at the right price.

Because this kind of conservatory is really a leisure building and cannot normally function or be thought of as a permanent house extension, it is accordingly expected to cost less. To keep prices down, the manufacturers have used mass-production techniques, which have reduced the range of options. In shopping for simple but well-designed timber or aluminium, single-glazed conservatories, the choice is more between different manufacturers than the styles of any individual manufacturer.

Planning the work

When it comes to planning the work on any extension, there are usually some fundamental problems that must be resolved. These relate to servicing the existing building either above or below ground and preparing suitable foundations in situations or circumstances often far from ideal.

It is important to remember that building services of any kind, be they plumbing, electrical or drainage, are there to accommodate the desired function of any living space. From a design point of view they are flexible and, if necessary, these should be moved rather than allow them to have a detrimental influence on the preferred layout or choice of site. Of course this can prove an extra and perhaps unforeseen expense, but the job is rarely as difficult or costly as you might think.

Plumbing – and particularly drainage – does have, for the average house owner, a certain fear of the unknown quality about it. Always seek expert advice at an early stage of the design to ascertain whether it is necessary to move or reroute services and, if so, what the problems and cost will be.

The best solution may be to leave pipework and even manholes and inspection chambers where they are. In this case provision

must be made for sealing around pipes if they run through the conservatory roof and refitting manholes with airtight, sealed covers. In any event, you should not allow the location of services, of whatever kind, to become a major motivating factor inhibiting the design or even the siting of the conservatory, if at all possible.

Matching the floor levels

Similar unwelcome pressures may be brought to bear on the choice of site by the apparent technical difficulty of matching the floor levels. Again, suitable adaption of the foundations and type of floor can avoid or overcome this obstacle.

If the ground level of the proposed site and the floor level of the room it is planned to adjoin are considerably different, a range of options is available. To have the floors of each room at the same level, either the conservatory floor – and supporting walls or piers – can be built up if it is too low, or it can be reduced by excavation if it is too high.

When the conservatory floor level is to be built up, this is usually done most economically by installing a suspended timber floor on joists, supported by brick or block walls or piers on a concrete footing. The advantage of this type of floor construction is that the new level can be brought up to exactly the required height. One of the drawbacks is that any suspended timber floor like this will tend to flex, if not fully supported, making ceramic or quarry tiles an unsuitable finish.

Do not forget that the material, style and finish of any walls, piers or columns built as part of the conservatory must be chosen carefully to blend in with the overall design.

Where the conservatory or ground level needs to be reduced to match an adjoining floor level, it will be best to use a solid, concrete foundation and floor. Since the ground will have to be excavated, any suspended floor, of the kind described above, would involve even deeper excavation. It is likely that any existing floor at this reduced or basement level will also be solid. This type of floor will take any finish – tiling of all types, wood strip or blocks, carpeting, and synthetic materials.

When excavating the ground for a conservatory, in most cases you can either build a retaining wall close to the extension to prevent the surrounding earth from infilling or clear the earth back some distance from the conservatory and possibly bank the ground between the two levels. In either case you have the chance to incorporate original design features, which will have to

Wooden steps lead down from a street-level conservatory to the basement-level garden. Trellis work provides a clever cover-up for the storage area beneath the conservatory.

include steps at some point around the conservatory to provide access to the garden. Make these a positive element of the design by planning them at the time you excavate, rather than adding them as an afterthought.

Whether you decide to build a retaining wall, or bank the ground, will depend on the available space. Obviously, building a wall will cause less disruption to the existing garden and take up less space than a bank. However, you should bear in mind the additional costs involved in building the former. Whichever method you use, it is very important that you leave a clear space around the base of the conservatory. If you do not, you will soon experience problems of damp around the floor.

If you have the space, there is a further option available. That is to make a feature of the area around the conservatory by laying out a terrace or patio, with steps leading from that to the higher level of garden.

The way current trends are moving should ensure the conservatory that starring role for which it has been groomed over many years – as an essential part of a new design while at the same time being the most natural and sympathetic addition to the old design.

The modern conservatory has the opportunity to become the hub of a new style of domestic architecture, offering far greater scope than the traditional enclosure until recently associated with its name. This potential has been achieved in part through the technical advances made in building designs and materials, and with a growing awareness of its new role as a glass-enclosed home extension. The same applies to apartments or large urban townhouses, in which cases the greenhouses are installed as extensions to the living space on large terraces or in roofs which are served by interior staircases or modified ladders. A number of manufacturers have designed attractive and inexpensive pre-fabricated attached greenhouses that fit the exact needs of city-dwellers.

Clever siting of this garden room close to lush outdoor planting gives the impression of actually being within a garden, but without the discomforts of cold and damp.

An Historical Interlude

The idea of the conservatory as we know it emerged at the end of the eighteenth century. The word had been in use since the late seventeenth century as a general synonym for greenhouse or orangery – a building in which tender plants were kept protected during the winter. Indeed, long after the domestic conservatory had been established, the word went on being used for a variety of greenhouses, publicly or privately owned, for domestic purposes or for the display of plants. Various writers tried to establish a distinction between conservatories and other forms of greenhouse, but were not really successful; the only generally distinguishing attribute of a conservatory was that it was used for pleasure rather than for practical purposes.

The fashion for building a glazed extension to the house, a hybrid area where house and garden interpenetrated, arose in England in the last years of the eighteenth century, but by the end of the Napoleonic wars had spread throughout northern Europe. The first half of the nineteenth century saw a continuous series of improvements in construction, in heating, and in cultivation. By mid-century, most countries could boast a variety of greenhouse and conservatory manufacturing firms, and most head gardeners on country estates were becoming proficient in the building and improving of glasshouses.

The domestic conservatory in its earlier years was, because of heating costs and the high cost of glass, exclusively a facility for the rich. By mid-century, however, partly as a result of new techniques, the price of glass had dropped radically, and the ability to own and maintain a conservatory spread down the social scale, until by the end of the century even a terraced house might be graced with one.

France and Germany pioneered the concept of the public winter garden: a conservatory, usually financed by a commercial company, which was to serve as a recreation and exhibition facility. In England, Paxton's 1851 Great Exhibition building, later re-erected as the Crystal Palace, inspired a wave of 'people's palaces' throughout the country. Eventually, local authorities came to see it as their function to provide this sort of facility for their residents, and the conservatory became a standard feature of public parks.

Of all this wealth of ornamental glasshouses, only a small proportion remains today. The commercial winter gardens and most of those in the public parks, have succumbed to the increased costs of heating and of repairs, and either have been demolished or lie derelict; changes of fashion in the present century swept away many domestic conservatories or at least removed their plant collections. Today, much of what survives is still in danger, even though the idea of the conservatory has been rediscovered.

The ancestor of the conservatory was the orangery, a structure designed for the cultivation of citrus fruits and other plants too tender to endure the winters of northern Europe. Orangeries began to appear about the middle of the seventeenth century, and were primarily distinguished from other buildings by their greater number of windows; they relied on masonry frameworks, and only during the course of the eighteenth century did they develop sloping roofs as a permanent feature; consequently, there were definite limits to their ability to admit light. Heating was provided by braziers or by stoves; the orangery shown here, illustrated in a Dutch work of 1670, was heated by two stoves (marked B). Two gardeners can be seen carrying one of the tubbed trees outdoors for summer display.

Compare this picture – of the heath house built at Woburn Abbey in the 1820s – with the foregoing. Increasing sophistication of design has meant that a far greater proportion of the walls and roof are composed of window glass. The glass is still set in small panes; plate glass was technically possible at this date, but with the high cost of glass and the unreliable quality of plate glass until the 1840s, it was better to use smaller, more easily replaceable units. Steam heating was being widely adopted by this time, shortly to be superseded by the hot-water boiler. The first experiments were being made with sprinkling systems, and run-off rainfall from roofs was being collected in tanks for use; but still the most convenient method of watering plants was that shown here – raising the roof-lights to allow rainfall to enter the building directly.

The illustration on the right and the one at the top of the opposite page show the competing styles in interior arrangement. This winter garden was erected in Paris in 1846 as part of the newly laid-out Champs Élysées; possibly because it was intended as a commercial venture – it charged admission, and functioned as a garden centre – it was arranged in the 'English' style, with plants either in tubs or confined to formal beds in which it was easy to view plants as specimens. After criticisms of the low roof and confined space, it was demolished the following year and replaced by a much grander conservatory, with curvilinear roofs.

This plan from a gardening manual of the 1820s, by Pierre Boitard, shows the alternative mode of arrangement, in which the conservatory houses a picturesque landscape. Characteristics of this style were: serpentine rather than straight paths, plants arranged in irregular masses rather than as readily distinguishable specimens, and, often, the use of climbing plants to disguise the columns and glazing bars.

Many conservatories and greenhouses were devoted to collections of particular types of plants, such as orchids or cacti, but one plant gave rise to a building type of its own. The Amazon waterlily, known in the last century as Victoria regia, was discovered in 1838, and wealthy landowners and botanic gardens competed to grow it and flower it for the first time. Sir Joseph Paxton built a Victoria house at Chatsworth in 1850 which became the prototype for later aquatic houses in its round pool. Shown here is the Victoria house in Brussels; originally erected in the Zoological Gardens in 1854, it was rebuilt and reinstated in the Botanical Garden in 1879 (it has since been moved again, to Meise). Octagonal in shape, its roof stood only 13ft (4m) high.

It was not only wealthy landowners and botanical gardens that invested in the creation of conservatories. The creation of giant glasshouses that were open to the public on a commercial basis was pioneered in Berlin at the end of the Napoleonic wars, but was practised on a wide scale only from the 1850s, when Paxton's Crystal Palace in London provided an obviously successful precedent. This view, left, of a winter garden proposed for Queen's Park, Glasgow, in the 1860s shows the main features of the public winter garden: a large domed structure, with most of its floor space given over to public promenading and social activities; a collection of ornamental plants, but comparatively few in number and mostly confined to tubs for ease in relocation; often a central feature like a fountain or rockwork. Winter gardens of this sort proliferated throughout Europe, but often proved excessively ambitious ventures for their parent companies, and have a low survival rate in consequence.

Shown, above is a view of the Imperial Wintergarden in Vienna, erected in 1822. Its architectural form is heavily indebted to the tradition of the orangery: apart from its immense window area, it resembles a neoclassical palace. This type of construction was on the point of becoming obsolete; gardeners had been looking for ways of ensuring the optimum amount of lighting throughout the day, and it was argued that this could be achieved by building curvilinear roofs that were parallel to the dome of the heavens. This was unfeasible in either brick or wood construction, for the thickness of the curved glazing bars necessary would have blocked out too much light; however, in 1816, the Scotsman J. C. Loudon patented a curved glazing bar in iron, which could create the desired effect. For the next quarter of a century, the most celebrated glasshouses, like the Palm House at Kew, were built in iron for this reason.

The results of using iron can be seen to advantage in this 1862 illustration, showing not only a roof divided into several curvilinear portions, but also a mass of fine decorative detail that would have been unstable if carved in wood. By this time, however, iron was falling out of use in conservatories; wood was not only cheaper, and easier to repair or replace without professional help, but gardeners had come to realize that curvilinear roofs – whose supposed necessity was the justification for building in iron – did not provide better lighting conditions than ridge-and-furrow roofs, or even simple span roofs, which could be built without difficulty in wood. So during the last half of the century, where iron was used for conservatories, it was not for functional reasons, but because of its ability to be shaped into delicate decorations.

The nineteenth century saw an unprecedented influx of exotic plants into Europe, and gardeners found themselves dealing with plants whose native growing conditions were unknown to them. Everyone's initial tendency was to be cautious, and to provide a greenhouse environment until it could be proven that a plant was hardy outdoors. Early conservatories, as a result, were planted with many plants – rhododendrons, camellias, myrtles – that are today familiar in the outdoor garden. By the 1870s, however, great experience and technological innovation meant that the bias was swinging in favour of genuinely tropical plants, often arranged in the picturesque fashion shown at the top of p. 37. This view, above, of a representative conservatory of the 1870s shows the effect of the palms and tropical foliage plants that were then coming into fashion.

The final blow to the reputation of iron for conservatory-making came in the 1870s, when the English glasshouse-maker W. H. Lascelles developed a process for bending wood under steam pressure (one of his models, displayed at the Paris Exposition in 1878, is illustrated below). It was thereafter possible to make curvilinear roofs out of wood; only now, of course, as curvilinear roofs were no longer considered functionally necessary, it was their ornamental value that was the motive for using them.

During the last quarter of the nineteenth century and the opening years of the twentieth, local authorities in virtually every European country installed conservatories in their public parks. These could range from houses devoted to plant collections, for both ornamental and educational purposes, to buildings modelled on the commercial winter gardens, with musical and recreational facilities. The expenses of repairs and heating have meant that many of these conservatories have been demolished in the mid- to late twentieth century, but often the larger structures are still standing. This conservatory, right, in the New York Botanical Garden, erected at the turn of the century, has recently been restored.

The story of the conservatory in the twentieth century has generally been one of decline. This Edwardian winter garden, below, made for James Kirkley of South Shields by the firm of Richardson and Co. of Darlington, illustrates some of the changes. The function of this conservatory is plainly as a social area: wide walkways create an open, spacious feeling; the plant collection has been reduced in size, and the arrangement of the furniture shows that it is now a background ornament rather than the centre of attention (note also the arrival of electric lighting). After the first world war, the conservatory was displaced by its rivals, the sun deck and the swimming pool (some conservatories were converted into pools); the major manufacturers found themselves reduced to making commercial greenhouses and glazed roofs for garages. Well before mid-century, more conservatories were being demolished than built, but in the 1950s a shrewd observer might have seen, in the German fashion for indoor planting in offices, the beginnings of the trend that was to bring the conservatory back into popularity.

The Conservatory Look – Inside and Out

If you lack the space and/or the necessary finances to build a garden room on to your house, the classic conservatory 'look' can be brought into almost every area of the home by means of clever colour scheming, decorating and accessorizing.

The primary aim is to create the impression of lush vegetation; dappled sunlight filtering through leaves, the filigree affect of ferns and vines, the sharp contrast found in flowers and exotic

A fresh clean look for a modern living room. Masses of foliage plants are strikingly offset by the stark white decor to give a garden room 'look' to a city home.

plants, fruits, birds, and even butterflies. For inspiration, look first at real conservatories and hothouses. Pay a visit to a local stately home or botanical garden, read all the articles you can lay your hands on, and study nearby attractive gardens.

Colour is terribly important and to be realistic, the scheme will have to be based on tones of green, contrasted with clear yellow possibly, to echo sunlight, or blue to simulate a summer sky. For a traditional Victorian look, use sparkling white paintwork – and for a more modern mood consider the warmer tones of natural wood. Alternatively, many wallpaper manufacturers are producing bamboo-trellis or plant-effect wall coverings which instantly create a conservatory atmosphere.

To control light and shade dispense with traditional pencil-pleated curtains and use blinds instead – the slatted vertical or horizontal Venetian type, or home-spun textured rattans. Or try delicate voile Austrian or festoon blinds to add a dainty, airy feel to a 'conservatory' room.

Lush vegetation, rush matting and the Colonial-style furniture and a ceiling fan – not forgetting the colourful caged bird – all combine to create a 'conservatory' in an ordinary living room.

The most important feature, however, will be plants. Use real ones where you can but be prepared to cheat a little if necessary – the modern plastic, silk or fabric flowers and foliage can be stunningly realistic when positioned with a little bit of thought. Mirrors used with careful planning will reflect, and apparently magnify, the amount of foliage as well as bringing illumination to an otherwise dark corner. If lack of light is a real problem, then bring in the artificial kind, with spotlights – both down- and up-lighters.

Finally, the 'conservatory' must be finished with a few carefully chosen accessories and pieces of furniture.

Room by Room Ideas

A dark basement corridor, festooned with pipes, or a narrow hall can quickly be converted into a verdant 'conservatory'. The simplest way is to choose a flowing floral or foliage design wallcovering to paper the walls and ceiling. Then paint the pipes, plus any skirtings, door and window frames to match the tracery on the wallcovering. To emphasize the conservatory theme, use a contrasting paint colour on the doors. If the ceiling is very high, divide the wall about one third of the way up with a dado rail, if none exists, by tacking on simple wooden quadrant or picture-frame beading. Decorate the wall above the division with a leafy or flower-patterned wallcovering and tack ordinary garden trellis to the lower part of the wall. If the trellis is to stand out boldly to contrast with a strong coloured background paint it white, and to offset white or a neutral coloured background paint the trellis in a bright clean colour.

Alternatively 'marble' the bottom of the wall with paper (or a painting technique called marbling) to imitate conservatory skirt walls and tack trellis to the top half. In a well-lit situation, real ivy or vines might be trained up the trellis, so long as it is fixed with battens or wooden cubes which hold it away from the wall slightly to allow plants to climb.

If there is a rather uninspiring blank wall at the end of the hall or on a half-landing, a false conservatory window can be created. Cover the wall with a piece of mirror or use self-adhesive mirror tiles, and then light from above with spotlights or pelmet lighting, and fix a plant-filled window box to the wall just below the mirror. If the area is rather narrow, cover the entire wall from floor to ceiling with mirror and group a collection of plants, dramatically lit, in front. In both cases trellising or a rattan screen would be a possible addition.

Glass shelves laden with plants are a pretty way of disguising an ugly view. The plants will thrive in a well-lit situation creating a living 'curtain'.

A well-lit window with a dreary view or an outlook on to a blank nearby wall is an ideal place to display a collection of trailing, creeping and upright plants; but ensure they will be protected against frosts on cold winter nights – if possible, the window should be double-glazed. Using metal bathroom shelf fittings, fix glass shelves, at suitable intervals, right across the window. In a windowless room such as an interior bathroom, combine this idea with the false mirror treatment and substitute fake foliage for the real thing.

Bathrooms are usually ideal places in which to recreate a mini hothouse atmosphere, and there are many humidity-loving plants such as ferns which can be displayed here. If the room is large enough, try to divide the lavatory from the rest of the area

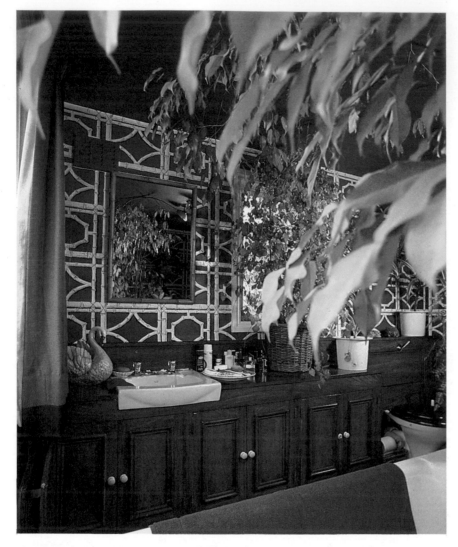

Trellis-like wall-covering and a jungle of plants transform a bathroom into an unusual room.

with open shelves on which to display a variety of plants, as well as pretty bathroom accessories. If space is at a premium, use an openwork screen of trellising instead, and either hang plant containers of trailing plants from it or train fake climbers through it. Bathroom windows are occasionally screened with often rather unattractive frosted glass, so the previous window shelving idea could be adapted to make the outlook more attractive. Trellis can be fixed to a frame that snugly fits the window opening, but removes easily for window cleaning and opening.

There are numerous ceramic tile designs on the market for walls which simulate a floral border or window box look, and these can be used to their full potential to create an impression of hothouse luxury. Some ceramic ranges incorporate exotic and tropical plants and palms, and it is often possible to buy special panels of tiles, which have trailing trees, or other foliage, as an essential part of the design. Place these panels in such a way so the leaves seem to be dipping into the bath water or basin, and emphasize the effect further with real or fake plants in front of the panel.

In many rooms, including the dining room, hall, bathroom, landing, kitchen and bedroom, a dull plain wall can be brightened up beyond belief by a mural or wallpainting. If you are artistic, then it is easy to design and paint your own – look at classical designs and illustrations of leafy vistas and translate them on to your wall area. If this seems a little ambitious try a gently rolling landscape with just a leafy background, or a simple arch through which sky can be seen, and with plants 'growing' up the side of the arch. Draw out your design on squared paper, then square up the wall on a proportionately larger scale, and transfer the picture, square by square, on to the wall. If both of these sound too daunting, consult a professional mural painter.

A clever way of dividing a room without losing available light. The suspended shelving provides a base for a screen of plants while the floor-level radiator rapidly disperses draughts from the doorway.

There are also various short cuts to creating an attractive wall painting: ready-made murals can occasionally be bought by the metre; a collage of plants and leaves, collected from magazines and catalogues, can be cut out, stuck to the wall area, and then varnished over, and stencils of plant and leaf shapes – either purchased or homemade from a piece of stiff card – can be used to great effect.

Large open-plan areas can be effectively divided visually, so the separate functions can be carried out in relative privacy: dining areas divided so the stove and sink are not immediately obvious from the dining table; a sitting or dining area partially divided from the hall or front door, when the main downstairs room has been made open plan with the hall; a dressing area in the bedroom, partially hidden from the bed or sleeping part of the room; and a long living/dining area partially made into two. These separate areas can be created without losing the overall impression of space and light by adapting the conservatory look for the purpose. Use gothic-style arched wooden dividers, or rattan or bamboo screens – even trellis screens mounted on a frame, or use pierced hardboard in a filigree effect. For a more simple division bamboo poles, slender wrought iron grilles, and copper or other metal tubing can form an open trellis for displaying climbing and trailing plants.

Furnish to Taste

The correct furniture is essential when creating a 'conservatory'. Look at garden catalogues and brochures, and visit garden centres to find furniture which will 'bring the garden indoors'. Junk shops, builders' yards, jumble and garage sales can also provide unusual finds which can be adapted to make plant tables, containers or display stands. Look at the various items on offer with a clinical eye, and try to appreciate their full potential – it is often possible to take a large piece of furniture such as a dressing table to pieces which can be used for several purposes. Old dressers, stripped and sealed or white-painted make good plant stands – use trailing and climbing plants and, in a kitchen or dining room, perhaps a selection of decorative herbs.

Old bamboo tables, whatnots, 1930s tiered cake stands, sewing machine treadle bases – all of which make unusual plant stands – can often be found in secondhand shops. Marble or tiled-topped washstands are particularly suitable to use as plant tables, as the surface is already stain and water resistant, and many an old rather unexciting but serviceable sideboard can be given a new lease of life with a tiled top (or protected with a sheet of glass) and covered with a mass of greenery.

In a room with a bay window, a conservatory area can be created using cane chairs, with comfy cushions upholstered in a crisp green and white leaf design, or a trellised floral: choose natural colours and green or autumnal colours and avoid bright florid tones. Add a glass-topped cane table, perhaps lit from beneath, and mass a collection of plants below and on top. If required this area can be divided from the rest of the room with a cane or rattan screen.

Original white wrought- or cast-iron furniture will give an Edwardian or Victorian flavour or buy modern cast aluminium copies. For an *art deco* look, spray wickerwork bedroom chairs of the period in white or a pastel colour. In a modern setting use natural canvas 'film director's' folding chairs with a simple cane or wooden table.

Hidden lighting dramatizes an attractive grouping of plants while mirror-lined walls reflect the overall effect.

Accessories

Smaller items can be used to enhance a conservatory corner, or to hold plants and flowers: an old commode with a china container or old hip or slipper baths make unusual and attractive plant holders. The conventional jug-and-basin set from a washstand may be a bargain buy because of a chip or crack, but when planted up it can become an ideal mini indoor garden.

An intriguing mix of plants and containers will create an indoor garden around almost any window.

50

Outside

Construction of a roof garden is another possible way of simulating a conservatory. It could be partly glazed to protect tender plants, or incorporate a small greenhouse. Flowers could be planted in pots and instead of real grass you could use synthetic lawn, bought by the yard. Garden furniture would allow you to enjoy such an area to the full. But – and it is a big but – there are several problems to overcome. There must be adequate access, the roof must be strong enough to carry the weight of pots, earth, plants, any construction, furniture and people, and an adequate drainage system must be provided. These factors are so important that you must consult a builder, architect or surveyor, who will also advise you whether planning permission is necessary.

Balconies, so long as they face the right way and get enough light and sun, can be converted to make ideal mini-conservatories. It may be necessary to install a windshield on one or both ends, with glazed sliding windows on the front, and some form of overhead protection. A simple awning might be sufficient, or a construction of reeded glass or transparent ridged plastic, suitably angled so rain and snow can drip easily away. In some cases, a permanent roof structure with proper drainage gutters may be essential.

Adequate access to the balcony is an important factor and remember that total enclosure prevents quick escape from a fire. If the balcony is on the front of the house, you must also consider what your proposed treatment will do to the overall look of the facade. You may also find – if you live in a block of flats for example – it is not possible to make any form of closed or permanent structure because of clauses in the lease or complaints from neighbours (particularly those living beneath you). If the house is in a conservation area or is a listed property, you may not be able to make changes that alter the essential architectural style. Whatever you wish to do you may have to apply for planning permission, and you will most certainly have to conform to the building regulations, so check with your local building department or planning office for advice before commencing. Permission may also be necessary if you propose to install or alter a porch or carport, so do ask for help and guidance before doing any construction work.

Porches can be enclosed with glass to make attractive and welcoming flower-filled entrances or you may be able to tack on a prefabricated one. Such additions will also give you the added bonus of a draft-free hall, but once again, permission may be necessary.

Carports and garden sheds can also be converted or used to make a simple conservatory when fully or partially glazed. Make full use of the roof construction and suitable translucent materials to let in light, but ensure it is strong enough to take hanging baskets – these can be the most effective way of displaying plants in this type of situation. Hanging baskets can be similarly used along a sideway – install a sloping transparent roof – or in balconies, porches, gazebos and greenhouses.

Make full use of any retaining or house walls; increase the available light, aid successful plant cultivation by painting the walls white or in a light colour such as blue or yellow or very pale green (think twice before doing this with old, mellow bricks or stone). Fix brackets for baskets to the wall, or window boxes, troughs or semi-circular baskets, or install adjustable shelves for trailing plants.

Gazebos, summerhouses and lean-to greenhouses, or extensions can be treated similarly. It may be necessary to bring most of the plants inside during the winter, particularly from a building which is at some distance from the house, although greenhouse heaters and oil stoves may be used. But always consider the hazard of winter frosts and snow and, if you are building from scratch or doing a conversion job, think of double-glazing as an investment. Scorching sun can be just as much of a problem, and some form of blinds or exterior awning may be necessary to lessen its effect on the plants in any of these structures. If installing new glazing, it is worth while considering the type of sandwich-pane which incorporates an internal Venetian blind.

All of these outside conversions or conservatory adaptations should be as well stocked with furnishings and accessories as the real thing, or as the indoor conservatory corners. Lighting, for example, to illuminate plants and accessories in the most dramatic way possible is an important priority. Garden lighting can be adapted for these exterior structures and cables will have to be of the safe exterior quality. Heating may be essential too, so consider piped power or extensions to an existing heating system. Furniture should be functional, flexible, but as pretty as possible, and again in keeping with the style of room you want to create.

Above all, having once made the decision to create a conservatory, you should be able to enjoy the result, and delight in the atmosphere you have created. Sitting among the plants and flowers to relax, work, or eat and drink should be the aim from the outset, so plan for comfort as well as elegance.

A roofed-over, open-sided extension becomes a conservatory with the aid of a cluster of plants and split-cane blinds.

Construction, Maintenance and Restoration

Once you have decided on the type and size of greenhouse or conservatory and selected its site, you must concentrate on the detailed planning and preparation work. Perhaps the most important aspect is to obtain any official approval that may be necessary (or at least to check whether such approval is required); this may take some time, so allow for it in your programme. It is also the time to decide exactly how much of the building you intend to do yourself, and how much (if any) you will sub-contract to professionals. Components and materials must be ordered and the site prepared for the construction.

Planning permission

In most countries, national or local planning controls exist to prevent piecemeal or unsuitable development taking place. These controls often regulate not only the building of houses, but any extensions added to them, including greenhouses and conversions that alter the house or apartment's exterior appearance.

Should you decide to ignore local building codes, recognize the risks in your locality as the local planning authority may be empowered to issue orders compelling you to undo any unauthorized development, and to restore the building to its original condition . . .

However, there is a brighter side to the planning maze too. Recognizing the fact that much small-scale development is inoffensive, building authorities generally allow for greenhouse alterations without the need for formal planning approval.

There are various conditions that your conservatory will have to satisfy to come within the rules, and these may vary from country to country. The main ones are those concerned with siting, size and extent. As far as the *site* is concerned, the building is likely to be permitted if it is at the back or side of your property; if it is at the front, or extends at the side beyond the building line in your street, then full-scale planning permission will probably be needed. Check with your local building officials.

The best course of action is to contact your local planning department and give them brief details of the work you propose to carry out. The department will then be able to tell you if you can proceed, or whether you need to apply for additional planning permission. *Never* take a chance and build without checking; the consequences could be very serious. Even if no action is taken in the immediate aftermath of such unauthorized construction work, you could well run into problems if you tried to sell your house.

A dream come true: an elegant conservatory in a sunny situation, completely finished, decorated, cleaned up and furnished with essential equipment, including roller blinds and a sink.

Note that if you live in a 'listed' building, in a landmark building, conservation area or within a National Park, planning permission will almost always be needed.

Building regulations

Apart from the intricacies of local planning controls, you will also need approval for the structure under the local or national building regulations. Whereas planning controls govern what kind of buildings can be erected (and where), building regulations are concerned with the way in which the job is done – in other words, that the standards laid down for structural safety and suitability of materials have been met. Even if a building such as a conservatory does not need planning permission, it must still satisfy the building regulations. These are usually administered by the same authority in your area that handles planning applications, although it will be a different department.

The kind of things building authorities check include:

(a) suitability of foundations, which must be strong enough to support the weight of the conservatory
(b) resistance to damp – with some methods of construction you may need to provide damp-proof courses in dwarf walls and beneath timber frames and panels
(c) fire resistance – the materials from which the conservatory is constructed will have to meet certain criteria, and you will have to provide a fire-resistant end wall to the building if it is close to the boundary of your property
(d) ventilation – if your conservatory covers natural means of ventilation to the rest of the house, it will itself have to be capable of allowing ventilation to take place through its structure
(e) alterations to existing drains, flues and so on – if these are necessary as part of the construction of the conservatory
(f) alterations to the structure of the existing house to provide access from it to the conservatory – you may need to form a new opening in the house wall and install doors or extra windows in it.

Unless you are building the whole conservatory yourself, using raw materials (bricks, mortar, timber and glass) you are going to purchase, you will find that the materials and design of the extension delivered by the manufacturer will meet the requirements of most building regulations. The manufacturer will provide all the necessary drawings and printed specifications for you to pass on to your local building inspector. You will, however, need to prepare some simple sketches showing the site of the conservatory in relation to the existing house, provide appropriate details of the foundations you will be laying, alterations to other structures, and so on. It is advisable to have a preliminary discussion with the local building inspector's office at an early stage so that you can be informed of any special points that will have to be satisfied before approval can be granted.

Foundations will usually need to be a simple flat concrete raft, a little larger overall than the perimeter of the conservatory. For some types of conservatory the edges of the raft may need thickening. If you wish to have bare soil within the conservatory for plants, you can lay strip foundations instead of a raft. The thickness of the foundations will be dictated by the building inspector, who has intimate knowledge of local soil conditions, but the conservatory manufacturer will also offer guidelines. If you intend to lay a floor-covering within the conservatory, you will have to incorporate a damp-proof membrane in the foundation slab (see p. 78) and top it with a screeding layer to provide a smooth flat surface.

Ventilation to the conservatory, and to any rooms in the house covered by it, must meet certain minimum requirements in order to satisfy the regulations.

Flues and downpipes on the external wall against which the conservatory is built may have to be moved, although with some types of construction it may be possible for them to pass through the roof at the point where it meets the wall. If the manufacturer of the conservatory you are installing recommends alterations to such pipes, discuss with the building inspector how the rerouting will be carried out.

Drains running underneath the conservatory can usually be left undisturbed, but if there is an inspection chamber (manhole) within its floor area it will have to be raised to the level of the conservatory's foundations – not in its entirety, but by building up its walls to the required level and then installing a new cover, level with the floor screed. Because the manhole will be inside the finished conservatory, it must be fitted with a double-sealed cover to keep out drain smells. The cover can be disguised by laying on it the same floor-covering as the rest of the room, but it must remain accessible in an emergency. Where the manhole falls directly underneath the wall of the building, it may be possible to bridge it with a lintel, but a better solution, if the extension cannot be moved to one side slightly, is to rebuild the manhole just outside the line of the walls.

Because a conservatory is not classed as a habitable room, most of the building regulations that apply to normal home extensions are not applicable. However, some thought should be given to the question of *insulation*, expecially if you hope to use the room as more than just a lean-to greenhouse. Double-glazed window and roof sections instead of single will reduce the amount of heat loss (but can cause condensation problems; check with the manufacturer), and you might consider having insulated cavity walls up to sill height instead of glass down to ground level. Of course, if you intend to use the conservatory as a sunroom in any but the hottest weather you will need to install some form of heating (see pp. 90-102).

As mentioned earlier, you may want to modify an existing opening in the house wall, or create an entirely new one, to provide *access* to your new conservatory. If this involves more than the removal of brickwork beneath an existing window in order to create a door opening of the same width, you will have to install a load-bearing lintel in the wall to span the new opening, and you will need to consult with the building inspector about its type and size.

There is one last point to remember about the whole subject of obtaining official approval for your conservatory. You should *not* start work until you have obtained all the necessary permissions in writing. This may take several weeks from the date of application (and if full planning consent is needed, rather longer) so be sure to allow for this when you plan your work schedules.

Ordering components

Having obtained approval, and if you are buying a prefabricated conservatory, now is the time to confirm your order, after making one last check that all items can be located exactly where you want them to be – positions of doors and opening vents, for example, may not be alterable later on – and that the specifications are correct. Complete the order form and ensure that you have the necessary financial resources to pay for everything on or shortly after delivery day.

If any of your requirements for the conservatory structure are unusual, or the site on which it is to be built an awkward one, call in the manufacturer's local representative for advice before placing a definite order – he will have far more experience of such problems than you, and will be able to solve them fairly easily.

When you place your order, you should receive full details of the size of foundations needed for the building (precise details of their thickness will, of course, have been specified by the local building inspector). This will give you sufficient time to prepare and excavate the site and lay the foundations (see p. 69) before the components arrive.

Before the components arrive, make sure that you have cleared a suitable area for them to be unloaded and stacked ready for use. Unless the weather is particularly bad there is no reason why they should not be stored in the open, otherwise move the car out of the garage and store everything there. Not only will everything be under one roof but also it will be protected from the unwelcome attentions of vandals or sneak thieves.

The manufacturer should send a full list of parts, which you should check off as they are unloaded. Pay particular attention to small components such as bolts, brackets and clips, even door furniture; nothing is more irritating than to reach a particular stage of the assembly and to discover that a small but vital item is missing. . . When you are satisfied that everything is present and in good condition, sign the delivery manifest. Lastly, be sure that the assembly instructions are included (unless they have been sent at an earlier date) – be prepared to study them carefully for at least a couple of days before you start work. This will give you time to double-check any points you are unsure of with the manufacturer and to familiarize yourself completely with all the components.

If you are building a conservatory from scratch, you are likely to be ordering materials and components from a number of different sources. Shop around carefully for the best prices, and always ask for discounts (particularly on the major items like timber or aluminium frame members, glass and concrete), also stress the importance of keeping to promised delivery dates – there is nothing worse than being held up by the non-arrival of supplies from one source when everything else has come. Use your working drawings and plans as an inventory, marking off every component as it arrives. Information on ordering materials is given in the next section.

Ordering materials

Whichever type of conservatory you are putting up, you will be constructing foundations which will need quite large quantities of raw materials – hardcore to consolidate the subsoil, and concrete to form the slab or strip foundations. At this juncture you must decide whether to tackle the job yourself or subcontract it to a local builder and, assuming that you choose the former course of action, it is time to do the estimating.

A typical slab foundation is likely to consist of 4in (100mm) of well-rammed hardcore (broken brick or concrete) on which the slab of concrete 100mm thick is laid). To calculate hardcore requirements, measure the area of the site. In imperial measurements, work in feet and divide the area figure by three to obtain the volume in cubic feet. In metric measurements, the area in square metres should be divided by ten to obtain the volume in cubic metres, rounding it up to the nearest cubic metre. Remember that a cubic metre is roughly 36 cubic feet.

You can order hardcore from most builders' suppliers, or from demolition contractors. Specify what you want it for, and ensure that it does not contain any soil or vegetable matter, which can decay and leave voids in the hardcore layer that can lead to subsidence. Of course, you may already have enough suitable material available – perhaps from previous alteration work in your home, or from the excavation of paths and steps to make way for the conservatory.

You will also need some finer materials for 'blinding' the surface of the hardcore (filling in the gaps between the chunks). You can use ash, sand or gravel (aggregate) for this. If you are ordering the last two items for making the concrete, add 10 or 15 per cent to your order to allow for blinding.

You can either order a delivery of ready-mixed concrete for the foundation or hire a concrete mixer and do the job yourself. The former method certainly speeds up the job – you will have your slab laid inside half a day – and is probably the only sensible solution if you need a large slab. By mixing the concrete yourself, you can work at your own pace, perhaps doing the job over several days, and this approach would be worth considering if you are laying strip foundations rather than a slab – it can be rather daunting having to cope with a delivery of ready-mixed concrete when there is much intricate laying and levelling to do, or if the access to the site is awkward.

There is unlikely to be any big cost advantage in either method – the extra cost of having ready-mixed concrete delivered will be offset by factors such as time saved and the necessity of having to hire a concrete mixer.

If you decide to mix the concrete yourself, you will need to order sufficient supplies of cement, sand and ¾in (20mm) aggregate for the base size of your conservatory. The correct formula for the cement, sand and aggregate mix for the foundation is in the proportions 1:2½:3½ by volume. If you order combined aggregate-sand mixed with gravel, the proportions should be 1 part cement to 5 parts aggregate. To calculate how much of each ingredient will be required, you must first find the volume of the slab – the same calculation that was made earlier for hardcore. A slab with an area of 215ft^2 (20m^2) and a thickness of 4in (100mm) requires a volume of 72ft^3 (2m^3). To produce this volume of concrete you will need 11 bags of cement, just under 1½ tons (1440kg) of sand and 2⅓ tons (2330kg) of aggregate – or 3¾ tons (3770kg) of combined aggregate. Use the figures in the table below to calculate the quantities for other slab volumes (a calculator will be helpful here).

Amount of materials required to make 1m^3 of concrete

Material	Proportion	Weight/Volume
Cement	1	5½cwt (5.6 bags*)
Sand	2½	14cwt/⅔yd^3 (720kg/½m^3)
Aggregate	3½	23cwt/1yd^3 (1165kg/¾m^3)
Combined aggregate	5	37cwt/1⅓yd^3 (1885kg/1m^3)

* each bag of cement yields 0.24yd^3 (0.18m^3) of concrete

For a job of this size it is advisable to order an extra 10 per cent of the bulk materials, to allow for waste and any slight inaccuracies in your measuring, estimating, and laying.

Order cement as near to the time of using as you can; it should not be stored for more than a week or so, as it can begin to harden in the bag. Store the bags flat and close together on a raised platform of boards (or at least on a plastic sheet) in a dry shed or garage. If you have to store it outside, again use a raised platform, and cover the bags tightly with a plastic sheet tied down or weighted in place.

Store sand and aggregate in separate heaps, if possible on a hard surface, and cover each with a plastic sheet to prevent the wind from blowing dust about, and rain from washing the finer matter away. If the heaps have to be left in the road, make sure they are neat, guarded by warning lamps at night, and that the material does not block the gutters – lay a board at an angle up against the kerbstone before the material is tipped into the road.

Remember that you will also need some formwork to contain your concrete as it is laid. This means outlining the slab with stout timber planks placed on edge and held in place with pegs to which the planks should be nailed. Use timber at least 1in (25mm) thick and at least as wide as the slab depth – 6in-(150mm-)wide boards are ideal for a slab 4in (100mm) thick. The pegs should be about 1¼in (32mm) thick, and about 12in (300mm) long, and need to be driven into the ground at corners and at about 3ft (1m) intervals. Round wire nails are ideal for fixing the boards to the pegs. You can use any sawn timber for the formwork; it can be cheaply bought from demolition contractors. To prevent the concrete from sticking to the boards, coat their inner surfaces with a release agent (available from builders' merchants) or with engine oil.

If you decide to use ready-mixed concrete, tell your local supplier what you want the concrete for, how much you need (rounded up to the nearest ¼m³ – rather more than ¼yd³) and whether it is to be discharged directly onto the site where it is needed (unlikely, unless you have excellent access to your premises). He will be able to advise you on the correct specification for the job. If you're ordering a large quantity, it is advisable to ask for a retarder to be added to the mix; this will delay the setting time, giving you more time to move it to the site and lay it in place before it starts to set.

At the same time, finalize the time of delivery, for you must be ready for it and have enough helpers and equipment to move it to the foundation site quickly. Each cubic yard (metre) of concrete fills 20 to 25 wheelbarrows, so you will need plenty of willing friends and neighbours on hand. If you have an awkward site for access, make a point of mentioning this in advance – mixer trucks are long, wide, tall and heavy!

If you are buying a prefabricated conservatory you will need little more for the job, but if you are building from scratch, you will need timber or proprietary metal glazing bars for the structure, glass or alternative glazing material, such as sealed units or polycarbonate sheeting, fixing devices, such as masonry bolts, nails and screws, flashing and damp course strips, sealants, and so on. The glazing bars and the glass are expensive items so it is worth sending your drawings to at least two suppliers to obtain quotations before placing the order.

When ordering timber glazing bars, either buy a weather-resistant species such as western red cedar or make sure that the wood has been pressure-impregnated with preservative. With aluminium types, you may have a choice of weatherproofing; some have synthetic rubber gaskets to hold the glass in place, while others (notably roofing bars) have a built-in flashing strip that is pressed down onto the glass surface to form a weathertight seal. Make sure that standard lengths are long enough for your purpose, otherwise you may have to order specially-made lengths. Also, ensure that you order sufficient fixings for assembling the structure, and discuss any special fixing problems with the supplier well in advance.

Tools are just as important as materials. Make sure you have all the tools necessary for the work, from shovels and spirit levels for laying concrete to saws for cutting components, and drills and screwdrivers for making the fixings. Check that cutting tools are sharp and that you have new masonry and twist drills of the right sizes – there is nothing worse than trying to make a fixing with a blunt or wrong-sized drill. For the repetitive work – mixing concrete or cutting intricate joints – hire equipment for the duration of the job. If you do not possess the right access equipment for completing the framework (such as ladders and scaffolding), or for fitting the glazing and roof flashings in position, then this too can be hired.

On the question of access, safety is all-important – a fall through a glazed roof could be very serious. Whereas the roof structure of some prefabricated conservatories is strong enough to support your weight on a roof ladder or crawling boards, on others it will be necessary to work through openings in the framework. If you have any doubts about weight restrictions or any other problems of access during the construction do ask the manufacturer for advice. Clearly, however, a stout access platform is safer than rickety steps perched on orange boxes.

It is best to leave ordering the various panes of glass you will need until you have completed the framework of the conservatory. At that stage you will be able to take into account any slight inaccuracies that may have crept in during drawing and construction, or any alterations forced on you during the building work by site problems or other peculiarities. The exception to this is if you are installing sealed double-glazed panels. Here, you will have ordered in advance, and as they will be on the site you will be constructing the framework to match their sizes precisely.

When ordering glass, provide the glass cutter with a detailed cutting list, preferably in metric measurements to avoid mistakes, and make sure that you have specified the various types of glass you want for the different panels. For example, you may want wired glass for the roof panels and for wall panels below waist level, and plain glass elsewhere. With patterned glass, specify which way the pattern is to run. For shapes other than simple rectangles, supply a paper or card template, which you should first test in the framework for fit.

Finally, do not forget to order the glazing materials – putty, mastic, glazing beads or whatever is appropriate to the particular method of construction.

Natural shading against too much sun can be provided by deciduous shrubby trees or climbers. Far left: the tree (1) planted to the east will provide some shade up to midday, while those on the south (2) and southwest (3), will give shade from mid-morning to mid-afternoon, and from late afternoon to sunset, respectively. Left: a deciduous climber on a pergola built 12-16in (30-40cm) away from the glass will give shade from above, while the 4ft (1.2m) high shrubs shade the front.

Site preparation

Having ordered all the components and materials, and gathered together the tools and equipment, it is time to prepare the conservatory site. The first step is simply to clear the decks – it is likely that the site has been previously used as a sitting-out area, planted with flowers and shrubs or grassed. Mark out the approximate area of the building with pegs and string, shifting all moveable items such as garden furniture. Then dig up and transplant any shrubs or plants that you wish to keep, and cut and lift turf – if in good condition it can be used elsewhere. Lift all loose-laid paving slabs and stack them for re-use.

If the site is covered with solid paving, concrete or some other durable surface, you may have to break it up systematically with a pickaxe or, more easily, with a hired electric breaker – a kind of small pneumatic drill – and the material could be used as hardcore beneath the new foundation. If the paving or other material is solid and sound, it might be possible to incorporate it within the new foundation, but this will depend on the levels and whether you know its precise composition – it must, for example, be thick enough to bear the weight of the new building. This you will have to evaluate on-site, and if there is any doubt in your mind, play safe and do not use it.

If the subsoil is well compacted and has not been used as a growing area, disturb it no more than necessary, for it will need to be recompacted. If, however, the area was well planted, you will have to dig deeply to remove roots and, perhaps, stakes. Save the topsoil for use elsewhere in the garden (or for the planters within your conservatory) and then excavate the subsoil to approximately the right depth for your new foundation slab, ready for setting out. It is best to clear an area two or three feet all round the slab site to provide plenty of room for working.

Setting out is the process of marking out the site so that the foundation will be in the right place, the right size and depth, and at the correct level. To do this accurately, you will need a long builder's tape measure, a long straightedge of timber, a spirit level, a club hammer, some stout string, some 1in-(25mm)-square timber pegs about 12in (300mm) long and a builder's square. On a large site a water-tube level (see below) will be easier and more accurate than a spirit level.

You can easily make a large builder's square from pieces of 2 × 1in (50 × 25mm) timber with its sides cut to length in the proportions 3:4:5. Cut a halving joint to link the shorter two sides at right angles, check that they are square and then nail on the cross piece to form the third side. Making a water-tube level is even simpler – it is just a long length of clear plastic tubing filled with water. Provided both ends of the tube are open, the water level will always be the same at both ends; so, when tied to pegs at opposite sides of the site the tube provides an easy way of levelling the peg tops. The ends of the level can be sealed with corks when not in use, and ink or dye will make the water easier to see.

To begin the setting out, you must establish and work from a line – somewhere fixed from which to take all measurements and angles – such as the wall of the house. You can then drive pegs into the ground at each corner of your proposed slab, with a nail in the top of each peg to locate the corners exactly. Drive two masonry nails into a mortar course in the wall, exactly the same distance apart as the foundation slab width. Call these two points A and B. Now stretch a string line from A at right angles to the datum line, measure along it to locate corner C on the line AC and drive in another peg. Repeat this process from point B to locate corner D. Note that the strings are not attached to pegs C and D – they pass directly over the nail in each peg top.

Now measure the distance between C and D – it should be exactly the same as the length AB. To check that the area is square, measure the diagonals AD and BC, which should be the same. You can now fix a string line, crossing points C and D, again with its ends attached to pegs outside the slab area. These string lines can be moved during the work whenever they get in the way, but the outer pegs must not be moved. The pegs at corners C and D can also be moved when necessary, for they can be replaced accurately using the string lines for reference.

On irregularly shaped areas, work out from the datum line as before, taking measurements from the scale drawing of the base and driving in pegs at all corners and at intervals along curves.

Next, you must set levels accurately. The base of your conservatory needs to be dead level in both directions (unlike a drive, which needs a cross fall for drainage purposes). For a base against the house wall, the house damp-proof course (dpc) is probably the best datum level to take; this means that the top of your foundation will be level with the dpc and you will be able to link it to the damp-proof membrane beneath the final floor screed. Working from this datum level you can drive in other pegs at intervals across the site to act as level guides. Across short distances you can check that their tops are level with the datum level using the straightedge and spirit level; over longer distances it will be more accurate to use the water level.

Having set the level lines, you can now complete the excavation of the site to the correct depth for whatever thickness of hardcore and concrete is specified. Work systematically across the site, taking care not to disturb the level pegs as you dig round them, and measure down each peg to gauge the depth. Remove high spots and fill hollows, so that when you have finished, the bottom of the excavation is reasonably flat and level.

If you are digging for strip foundations instead of for a slab, the principle is similar, the only difference being that you will

Accuracy in setting out the site is of paramount importance. A builder's square, top left, is simply made: the dimensions given can be varied, provided the same proportions are used. Also easily made is a water level shown in use at the bottom left. In the centre is the method of marking out the rectangle for the base, while at the top right is a detail of the corner pegs. If you want to have a bed of soil in the conservatory for plants, you will need to make trenches for strip foundations. The setting out, using double string lines and profile boards, is shown at the bottom left.

need pairs of string lines along each side of the site to outline the trench widths. Again set level pegs along the line of each trench and check them back against your datum level.

As you dig, watch out for any buried services – drains, water and gas pipes, and electricity cables. If you find any, contact the relevant authority (building inspector, water board, gas company or electricity supply undertaking) for advice on protecting or rerouting them.

Obstacles on the house wall, the most likely being downpipes and soil pipes, should be dealt with at this stage. You will generally be able to reposition them (with the help of offsets and bends, where necessary) so that the wall area to which the conservatory is to be fixed is completely clear. In the case of soil pipes, consult with your local authority building inspector first.

Laying the foundations

Start this stage by setting up framework boards round the perimeter of the slab area, setting them accurately in line with the string lines and, using the spirit level, make sure that the top edges of the boards are level with the pegs in the site area. Butt-joint the corners of the formwork tightly to prevent the wet concrete from seeping out, and nail the boards to pegs driven into the ground outside the boards. If you have to place two planks end to end to make up the required length along one side of the site, again use a butt-joint, and back both planks at the join by a short length of timber nailed in place on the outside and wedged with an extra peg.

Now lay the hardcore to approximately the required depth across the slab area (or in the foot of the trenches for strip foundations). Tamp it down well with your heel and a stout length of heavy timber, such as a fence post used on end. Add more hardcore in any obvious hollows, and ram down any lumps that protrude from the overall level by more than about 1in (25mm). When satisfied that the hardcore is reasonably level and well rammed down, cover it with a blinding layer of sand, gravel or ash, making sure that any large gaps in the hardcore are well and truly filled.

On slabs larger than about 10ft (3m) in any one direction, the next job is to divide the area into bays with more lengths of timber. Not only does this make the job of laying the concrete easier, but also it has the essential purpose of providing *expansion joints*, which allow the slab to expand without cracking. Cut lengths of formwork timber to form the bays, and peg the first one in place. When the bay has been cast, a strip of softwood about ½in (12mm) thick should be sandwiched between the cast edge and the next bay, to remain permanently in place when the slab is completed.

If mixing your own concrete, use the same sized container for measuring all the materials; a heavy-duty 3 gallon (15 litre) bucket will be ideal, as a batch based on a bucket of cement will be a convenient size for hand mixing or feeding a small mixer. Use one bucket for cement and another for sand and aggregate, otherwise moisture from these materials will cause the cement to cake on the sides of the bucket.

Fill the bucket with cement, tap the sides two or three times to shake down the cement and then top up as necessary. Measure out sand and aggregate level with the bucket rim. Add only enough water to the mix to make it workable; after two or three batches you will be able to gauge exactly how much to add each time to give mixes that are reasonably similar in consistency.

If mixing with a shovel, measure out the aggregate into a compact heap, form a crater in the top and add the cement. Turn the heap until the whole pile is uniform in colour and texture, then form a crater in the top again and start to add the water. Continue adding until the wet mix is uniform in colour and consistency and has the right workability; test this by using a trowel or the back of the shovel to smooth the surface of the heap, which should, if correct, have a closed texture without any run-off of water.

When using a small mixer, set it up level and brace it to prevent movement. Then, either set up a board of plywood underneath its drum so that the mix can be poured onto it or raise the mixer high enough for its contents to be discharged directly into a barrow. Put half the aggregate and half the estimated amount of water into the drum and let it turn over for a while. Then add most of the cement and sand, continue mixing and add the rest of the materials in alternate shovelsful, keeping the mix fairly wet until nearing the end to ensure thorough mixing and to avoid the build-up of dry material on the drum sides. Leave the mix turning for about two minutes, then tip it out. Do not overload the mixer or leave it empty for more than about 15 minutes between batches, otherwise it will begin to cake up. If you will be away for longer than this, either hose out the drum or leave some aggregate and water turning in it to keep it clean.

When the batch is mixed (or when the lorry arrives to deliver the ready-mixed concrete), barrow each load to the site, running along planks and ramps set up in advance on poor ground or

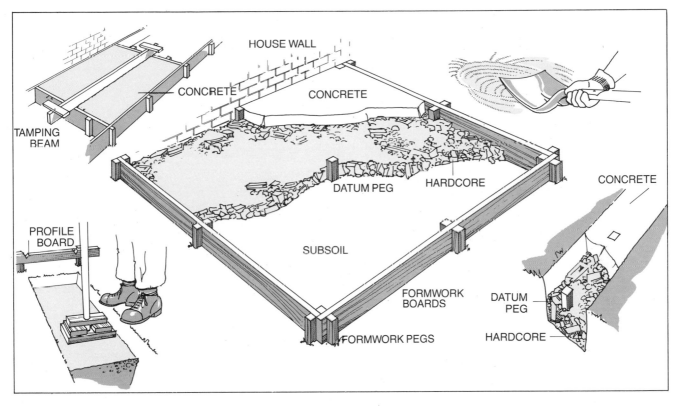

HOUSE WALL

CONCRETE

CONCRETE

TAMPING BEAM

DATUM PEG

HARDCORE

CONCRETE

PROFILE BOARD

SUBSOIL

FORMWORK BOARDS

DATUM PEG

FORMWORK PEGS

HARDCORE

across unpaved areas, and tip it into the formwork in a heap. Spread it out evenly with a rake and level it to just above the top of the formwork – about ½in (10mm) higher on a slab 4in (100mm) thick. Make sure that corners are well filled, and 'strike off' the surface by drawing a long straight-edged board across it to reveal any bumps or hollows. Slice off any excess concrete from the bumps with a shovel, and use it to fill any hollows.

The next stage, and one that is vital for success, is to compact the concrete to fill any voids and drive out air pockets. Compact the slabs with a tamping beam of 6 × 2in (150 × 50mm) timber, long enough to span each bay, and fitted with make-shift handles for ease of use – operating one is a two-person job. Use the tamper with an up-and-down motion, moving it along by about 1in (25mm) at each stroke – do not just scrape it along the tops of the formwork boards. If necessary add more concrete to fill hollows and to close any patches with an open surface texture – the latter is an indication that they have not been properly compacted. With trench foundations, use a home-made punner to tamp the concrete down level with the tops of the datum pegs (which should be carefully removed when the concrete level has been checked).

The sequence of laying the foundations. The centre illustration shows the formwork boards, their retaining pegs and the layers of hardcore and concrete. The detail, bottom right, shows a trench or strip foundation with its all-important datum pegs. At the bottom left, the hardcore is being tamped down and, above, is the method of working in bays to provide expansion joints, and the use of a tamping beam on the laid concrete. Smoothing the level concrete is shown at the top right.

Continue laying successive bays (not forgetting the expansion joint) or lengths of trench in the same way, carefully checking the levels until the foundation is complete.

You can, if desired, give the surface of the concrete a smooth finish, using a wooden float or the back of a shovel. However, if you are planning to lay a fine screed to take a floor covering when the conservatory is finished, simply leave it with the lightly rippled finish left by the tamping beam.

The concrete should now be left to harden and gain strength, but if it is allowed to dry out too quickly it will crack. This can be prevented by covering it for three days with plastic sheeting or damp sacking, weighed down round the edges. Wait a further three to four days before erecting the conservatory on it.

Constructing a prefabricated conservatory

With a prefabricated conservatory that has been carefully chosen to take account of all the peculiarities of your home and the site, the actual erection should be little more difficult than assembling a rather large greenhouse. The manufacturers provide comprehensive installation instructions that include the order in which the component panels should be assembled, how to fix the structure to the base slab and house walls, how to install the glazing panels and other components to complete the building.

It is essential to read the instruction manual carefully and closely examine all the components – it is surprisingly easy to confuse similar-looking pieces when there are fifty or so spread out all over the drive. This could be done while the base slab is hardening. At the same time, check your tool kit to ensure you have everything required, and that all is in good working order.

The assembly sequence will vary according to the type of conservatory you have purchased. However, the following account, based on the erection of the popular aluminium-framed type with curved eaves, will illustrate many of the points common to all.

The first stage is to choose which end of the building is to have the access door to the garden, and to assemble the end frame components – usually simply bolted together. Do the same for the other end of the building, then offer up the end panels in position on the base slab – a helper will be required for this – and link them with the main waist-level rail, the bottom front cross rail and the main ridge bar, all running the length of the building. When this has been done, the basic frame will stand on its own and you will be able to add any other rails running parallel to those already

Having decided which end of your prefabricated model is to have the door, the next stage is to assemble the two end frames.

With the end frames in position on the base slab and the main waist-level rail bolted on, the front ridge bar can be fixed.

Once the alignment of the frame has been checked, the rear uprights can be drilled for fixing the structure to the house wall.

When the main ridge bar has been screwed to the wall, the latter can be chased out for fitting the flashing at the roof junction.

After the glazing bars have been inserted, the panes of glass for the roof can be slid into position. Complete each bay in turn.

The curved plastic glazing in each bay is fitted after the flat panes, sprung into place and secured with a glazing gasket.

Opening roof windows, hinged on the lip of one of the ridge bars, are generally slid into their bays from one end of the bar.

Assemble and fix the door frame; hang the door, checking for smooth operation, and then glaze it.

If all is well, fix the frame to the slab by drilling through the base rail and concrete, and screw it into expanding anchors.

71

fixed. To complete the skeleton, add the intermediate curved upright/roof sections at the correct intervals along the length of the building, bolting them to the horizontal rails and the top ridge bar.

Assuming that the base slab was laid truly level, the skeleton should now stand with its uprights vertical; check this with a spirit level, and if there are any discrepancies, pack thin strips of bituminous roofing felt or some other non-degradable packing under the bottom rails until the frame is standing square. You will now be able to see how true the house wall is; the side frames should meet it perfectly, but most likely there will be gaps and inaccuracies at several points. Most manufacturers supply a special flexible sealing strip to fit between the frame and the house wall to take up the discrepancies of fit, but if the gaps are more than about ½in (12mm) wide you will first have to fit preservative-treated timber battens or some other suitable packing material to the wall.

With this particular conservatory, the window and door frames help to square up the structure, so it is usually recommended that these should be fitted into the skeleton at this stage. You will probably have to slide in weatherseals and glazing gaskets first before screwing together the frame sections; it is then a simple job to offer them up into position and attach them one-by-one to the frame members.

The next job is to secure the frame to the house wall, by driving fixing screws through the rear uprights and into expanding metal anchor bolts set in the house wall itself. For a really firm fixing these should be set into the centre of a brick, not into the mortar courses. This is the last chance to make sure that the structure is standing square and level. Screw the main top ridge bar to the wall in the same way, and chop out a chase in the house wall just above it to accept the flashing that will seal the conservatory/house-wall junction (this may not be needed on a bungalow or any other one-storeyed building, where the roof of the conservatory fits under its overhanging eaves).

The glazing panels can now be fitted into place. Follow the manufacturer's instructions carefully for this operation, fitting the various panes in the recommended order and taking care to check the positioning of weatherseals and clips. Roof panes need particular care; as you offer up each one, slip one edge into the glazing bar to take the weight of the glass and then slide it gently into position. With the curved-eaves type, the curved pane is often of acrylic or some other plastic glazing material rather than glass, and is usually the last to be 'sprung' into place.

Opening roof windows are usually hinged on a lip in the ridge bar or on one of the main transverse roof bearers, and may have to be slid into place from one end of the building before being positioned in the correct bay.

Once all the glazing is in place, the door and its frame can be made up from the various components and hung. Check that this and any opening windows or vents operate smoothly. The conservatory can then be permanently fixed to its base by drilling down through the base rail into the concrete, inserting expanding anchors and driving in the fixing screws. Finish off by piping a bead of silicone sealant around the inside of the frame where it meets the base, and check the seal in the junction between the house wall and the sides of the conservatory, again using a flexible sealant to close any slight gaps.

Although details vary, most conservatories capable of do-it-yourself erection will have a roughly similar sequence. The key lies in following instructions to the letter and working methodically through them step by step. If you do run into difficulties, however, you can always contact the technical department of the makers of your particular kit. They are always willing to help, and some may have a local representative who will give you advice.

Building your own conservatory

If you are building your conservatory in its entirety, you will certainly need a great deal more ingenuity and skill than if you were erecting it from a kit.

You are most likely to be working in timber so, provided you have accurate drawings to work from, the construction of the framework will require only normal carpentry skills and careful workmanship. With any timber structure, even if the wood has been preservative-treated, it is essential to provide a damp-proof course between the slab itself and the bottom of the wall sections; this can best be done by setting the bottom framing timbers on a strip of the same dpc material that is used for house walls (if necessary it can be trimmed down to width). Wall fixings require the same care as those for a kit building, as will attention to weatherproofing where the structure abuts the house; however, for anyone competent enough to contemplate building a conservatory from scratch none of these points should pose any insuperable problems.

One advantage of building your own conservatory is the ease with which minor adjustments can be made to the structure as the work progresses to take account of any unseen problems – in

An energy-efficient sunroom under construction. Designed for the harsh winter climate of Wisconsin, it features devices for energy saving, including an air-transfer fan in the house wall for pulling in warm air from the extension, and a baseboard vent and duct system for returning cold air. The outer walls will be finished in wooden cladding to match the house, and the pair of sliding patio doors will give access to a wrap-round wooden deck for summer use.

Labels in the illustration:

RAFTERS
WALL PLATE
WINDOW FRAMES
CORNER POST
OPENING WINDOW
SILL
FIXED GLASS
dpc STRIP
WIRED GLASS
RAFTERS
FASCIA
GUTTER BRACKET
CORNER POST
SOIL
TURF
PLASTIC SHEET
DRAIN PIPE
HARD CORE
HINGED DOORS

particular, while working round obstacles such as downpipes and soil pipes. It is a comparatively simple matter to box out the framework round the pipes and other obstructions, and to use flashing strips or cut-outs in the glazing panels to complete a seal round them.

With a self-build conservatory it is wise to minimize the amount of future maintenance work by using as many professional tricks as possible. Two obvious ones concern the decorative treatment of the timber and the bedding of glazing panels. It is a big mistake to paint or varnish the woodwork; this may be easy enough if you pretreat the frame as it is and before the glazing is in place, but it will be much more difficult in future years. It is far better to use one of the preservative stains; these products come in a wide range of colours, and because they do not form a surface film on the wood, there is no risk of flaking and cracking. When the frame needs redecorating, simply wash down the surface to remove dirt and dust and then brush on a further coat. When glazing the conservatory, avoid putty, which will crack and allow leaks to appear as the years go by. Instead, bed all the panes on non-setting mastic which remains flexible and gives a far more permanent waterproof seal.

A comparatively easy way of designing and building your own wood-frame conservatory is to use off-the-shelf windows and hinged doors. Buying these items will simplify much of the construction, leaving you to deal with the roof and its guttering, the corners, soakaway, glazing and decorating.

Whatever type of conservatory is being built, remember to make provision for the disposal of rainwater from its roof. Many kit conservatories have integral drainage channels in the roof, and downpipes in the wall uprights, but with a self-build conservatory incorporate gutters and downpipes (probably in maintenance-free plastic) either on the outside of the structure or concealed behind fascia panels and frame uprights. In each case, take the downpipe into a gully, sunk below ground at a suitable point, to trap debris washed off the conservatory roof, and then run an underground pipe to a soakaway sited at least 16ft (5m) from the house (ascertain the precise distance from your local building inspector). Alternatively, install a water butt to collect the water.

Once the building is complete, run in any plumbing and electrical services you require. The former may be no more than a cold tap for plant watering, and it is quite simple to run a branch pipe from a convenient supply pipe to the rear wall of the conservatory, where a wall-mounted tap can be fitted. If you want to extend your heating system to provide radiators within the conservatory, more extensive work will be needed.

If a light fitting and perhaps a power point or two are all the electrical services required, these can easily be run as extensions from the house's existing circuits. But for more complex installations – for example, electric space heating – it is far better to wire up the conservatory on its own separate lighting and power circuits and to provide additional electrical protection for these with earth-leakage circuit breakers (pp.100-102). Make sure that all the fittings are of the splashproof type if the conservatory is going to be used for growing plants.

Fitting out

Once the structure is complete, you can turn your attention to the fitting out – all the extras that turn the new room from a shell into something functional and attractive. Probably the most important thing to consider is the floor, and how you treat this will depend on the use to which the room is put. If it is simply to be a sitting-out area, almost any floor-covering can be chosen – although the necessity for a hardwearing surface that is easy to keep clean should be borne in mind. Popular choices include vinyl flooring, tiles (vinyl or ceramic) and even woodblock or parquet flooring. Whatever you choose, lay a damp-proof membrane (heavy-duty polythene sheeting or a brush-on coating) over the slab and then lay a thin screed of fine concrete over the top to create a smooth, damp-free surface. However, you may

The importance of the floor as a unifying element is evident in this beautiful conservatory. In order to achieve such a perfect finish, the screed must be perfectly level. Although the floor illustrated is highly polished marble, a not dissimilar effect can be had by using lino tiles which are, of course, far less expensive.

Staging and shelving can be cheaply made or bought as components which are easily fitted together. Illustrated here is a selection of possible arrangements. Top left: *slatted staging, made of wood, which can be constructed to the working height you prefer;* top centre: *free-standing wooden-shelving;* above: *steel racking, quickly bolted together, is strong but not particularly attractive in a conservatory for living in;* far left: *a slatted timber shelf supported by metal brackets;* left: *adjustable shelving system, using slotted uprights.*

wish to go to the other extreme and use the conservatory more as an indoor garden, in which case the most suitable materials are likely to be quarry tiles or some form of decorative paving, laid in a mortar bed on the base slab. Either way there is a wide choice of materials available to suit both taste and budget.

Having attended to the floor, plan what provision you want to make for plants. What you do depends on the type and number of plants you want to display – you may fancy nothing more elaborate than a few floor-standing containers, but for a more comprehensive display you will need shelving or staging, and probably some plant supports.

Many conservatory manufacturers offer their own staging kits, ranging from simple free-standing trestle-type units to more elaborate shelf fittings that can usually be clipped at intervals to the building's uprights. If they suit your requirements purchase them, for their cost will be included in the price of the structure, enabling you to arrange your display in the minimum of time.

If you wish to buy or make your own shelving and staging, start by deciding on what materials you prefer. Metal units can be built up from bolt-together components; there is a wide range of semi-industrial shelving and storage systems to choose from, and the result will be strong and hard-wearing, if not particularly attractive. However, wood is likely to be the first choice for most people because it is readily available, comparatively inexpensive and easy to work. Make sure, however, that the wood is either preservative-treated (with a product that will not harm the plants) or better still, is naturally durable – western red cedar is one of the best woods because it is strong yet surprisingly light.

Floor-standing trestles should be made with slatted tops so watering and planting spills can be easily dealt with. Legs should be braced to cope with the weight of plant pots and trays.

Taller free-standing display units can have solid or slatted shelves. Make sure that adequate support is provided to prevent sagging and it is also a good idea to tie such units to the walls of the house or sunroom to improve their stability.

If you prefer wall-mounted shelving, the simplest solution is to mount adjustable shelves on the house wall. The uprights can be

Shelving need not be as utilitarian looking as that in the drawing opposite. Here, brass and cast iron have been used to great effect to support a mass of plants. Of equal interest is the clever way in which the brass shelving has been used to link the access from the house to the extension along one side of the step.

79

screwed to wallplugs set in the masonry for a secure fixing, and the brackets are then slotted into place at the required height and spacing. As with trestles, it is best to make up slatted shelving and stand pots on shallow trays, but you can use solid shelves if you prefer. If you use man-made boards, employ only exterior-grade plywood – moisture will adversely affect any other type.

Depending on the construction of the building, you may be able to mount shelving on the uprights of the building itself. This is easiest if the uprights are wooden, but if they are metal you will have to drill pilot holes and fix the brackets with self-tapping screws (take care not to crack the glass or pierce any sealing gaskets). Remember, however, that shelving against the glass walls will make glass cleaning difficult and will also expose the plants to the maximum sunlight unless you have some sort of blinds fitted to shade them.

Soil-filled free-standing troughs, which can be moved around if necessary, can be used for planting at ground level. They will provide sufficient depth of soil for most of the species you want to grow (see pp. 145-185). The alternative is in-ground planting in a conservatory built on perimeter strip foundations rather than on a base slab. Here, the soil is cultivated and planted just as it would be inside a greenhouse.

Trailing wires or trellis can be added to assist plants to climb the walls or to snake their way across the ceiling. They can be fixed to the structure using screw-in hooks and eyes, but ensure that the fixings are firm – fully grown plants are surprisingly heavy, especially fruit-bearing species. Also, you must bear in mind the problems that will arise in cleaning and maintenance if the plants are trained over too much of the structure.

Also at this stage add any blinds or other forms of shading that will be attached to the structure of the building, as they will be difficult to incorporate once the plants are established.

Creating access from the house

Many conservatories will be built over an existing opening in the house wall – French windows or sliding patio doors, for example – in which case there may be no need for any modification to the access from house to conservatory. But if there is no access from the house, you can create a new opening.

The most likely situation is that there is already a window in the wall against which the conservatory stands. In this case it is a relatively simple matter to remove the window frame and the masonry beneath the sill, and to fit a door frame having the same

A good way of growing pots of flowers in a plant room is by building brick staging to a working height, and providing a recess for gravel. Here the bricks have been painted white, not only to increase the reflected light but also to make a contrast with the quarry-tile floor – itself a good covering for a room where there is likely to be a fair amount of moisture.

Creating access from the house to the conservatory is not a particularly difficult task where there is already an opening. Far left: the window and its supporting brickwork are removed and, leaving the existing lintel, replaced with a frame for patio doors. Left: widening a narrow door opening will require the insertion of a new full-length lintel before the brickwork is cut away.

width as the original window opening. The existing window lintel need not be disturbed, but if the dpc in the house wall is disturbed while fitting the door, it must be carefully reinstated.

Where there is no opening, or the existing opening is too narrow, more major structural work will be necessary. Basically, a new lintel will have to be set in the masonry to span the full width of the proposed new opening, and then the masonry will have to be cut away beneath it to create the new opening, ready for its door frame. If you are contemplating this kind of structural work, you must consult your local authority building inspector for approval of the plans before starting, for it is possible that such alterations could seriously jeopardize the structure of the house unless they are properly carried out.

Maintenance of new conservatories

A new conservatory will require relatively little maintenance to begin with, but it will give better service and last much longer if a proper routine is established. Probably the most recurrent problem will be cleaning the glass, especially on the outside. If the structure is strong enough to support the weight of crawling boards the panes can be washed down individually with a sponge or squeegee, but only climb on the roof if you are sure it will bear your weight *and* if you feel safe at heights – the consequences of a fall could be disastrous. For most conservatories it will be easier to clean the roof glass working from a step ladder set up at eaves level using a long-handled mop or sponge of the type used for washing floors. The surface can be rinsed off with a fine spray from a garden hose.

Metal-framed conservatories need comparatively little maintenance other than an occasional wash-down, which can be done while the glass is cleaned. Wooden-framed models need rather

Round concrete-cast blocks, forming a 'waterfall' of steps, make a natural-looking way up to a conservatory from a passage, the walls of which are of the same colour. The passage floor cleverly repeats the circular motif of the steps.

Maintaining the exterior of a conservatory roof requires careful attention to safety. Far left: a crawling board with load-spreading timber below it, supported by a bearer and adjustable prop inside the structure; left: a snow guard, which will also prevent loose tiles from sliding onto the glass roof; below, far left: temporarily repairing a cracked pane of glass with glazing tape; below left: a ladder lashed securely to a large hook firmly screwed into the fascia board.

more attention. Inspect the frame members and glazing bars at least once a year, looking for any signs of rot or areas where the finish needs touching up. Painted or varnished wood is likely to need localized attention annually, and comprehensive redecoration about every three to five years. Timber treated with a coloured preservative stain will need less attention – just a wash down and a fresh coat every two or three years.

Check too that the glazing is in good condition, and that there are no leaks in the mastic. Cracked glass can be temporarily repaired with proprietary glazing tape, but only complete replacement will make a satisfactory long-term repair if a pane is broken or badly cracked. Where putty has been used and crumbled with age, seal the leak with mastic or cover the glazing bar with a self-adhesive flashing strip as a temporary measure.

The house walls above a conservatory can be difficult to maintain because the building below impedes free access. Ideally, you should have maintenance-free plastic or aluminium-framed windows in such situations, with tilt-and-turn casements that can be cleaned from within the room. Walls should be of facing brickwork rather than of rendering, which will need repainting,

The outward-opening doors and windows of the conservatory opposite can be cleaned and maintained easily working from a low stepladder. The outside of the glass roof, too, can be managed from a short ladder, using a long-handled mop. Further access is possible from the window above.

and gutters should be plastic rather than cast iron. However, in a less-than-ideal world, you will probably have to gain access to this area at some stage, and the only really practical answer in most cases is to use a ladder to bridge the conservatory roof. This will mean setting it at a far shallower angle than is usual (or safe); to make the best of a risky situation be sure that the foot of the ladder is set against stout pegs so that it cannot slip, and try to use a long extension ladder with the biggest possible overlap between sections, to stiffen it and to reduce flexing as you climb. Mount carefully, and have an assistant to pass out your tools through an upstairs window rather than risk dropping them through the glass roof as you climb.

One last point concerns another safety angle. Any conservatory is at risk from objects falling onto its roof, even if toughened or wired glass is used. The two biggest dangers are loose tiles or slates sliding off the house roof, and heavy snow avalanching off its slopes. Guard against both events by fitting a snow guard to the house fascia so that it protrudes above the gutters.

Restoring old conservatories

If you have an old conservatory, restoring it to its original condition could, depending on the amount of work necessary, be a great deal cheaper than building a new one. First, carry out a survey of the structure. Then look at the state of the glazing and its bedding, check the soundness of the timber (even if superficially rotten) and, if of metal, the state of its structural steelwork. If there is any doubt about its structural safety, call in a professional builder or surveyor to give you a full report.

Unless you are very fortunate, you will probably be faced with complete reglazing, and a great deal of work on the framework. Start by removing all the old glass – if possible in whole panes, for some may be worth saving. If you have to break any glass, criss-cross it with self-adhesive tape first to stop splinters flying everywhere, and crack it with the minimum of force.

When the glass has been removed, clean out the glazing rebates with an old chisel to remove the original putty, fixing nails and clips. Cut away extensively rotten wood in timber-framed structures and join in new sections, otherwise let in patches of new wood or use a resin repair kit. If made of metal frames, wire-brush rust back to a bare surface, and fill any small holes and damaged areas with car-body filler. Larger areas of damage will be more difficult to repair without specialized help or considerable metal-working experience.

The next stage is to prepare the frame for reglazing. On timber frames that have been painted, thorough priming of all bare timber is essential, followed by an undercoat and at least two top coats of good-quality gloss paint. Where varnish was originally used, it is advisable to re-cover with yacht varnish or a similar product rather than with polyurethane varnishes, which tend to crack in exposed conditions and are difficult to revarnish. If the whole frame can be stripped back to bare wood without too much effort, redecorating with a pigmented-preservative stain will give a longer-lasting and lower-maintenance finish.

Clean, bare metal should be treated with a metal primer – calcium plumbate is recommended, but it does contain lead – and then painted with an undercoat and gloss.

The glazing can now be replaced. This is a good opportunity to fit wired or toughened glass (certainly in the roof and low-level panels, if not throughout). Bed the glass on beads of non-setting mastic, securing them with glazing sprigs or clips as appropriate.

Once this has been done, pay attention to the sealing between the conservatory and the house wall. If necessary, fit new flashing strips where its roof meets the house wall. This is best achieved by first fitting the centre pane in the final row of glass, and dressing the flashing down onto it, and then fitting the adjacent panes, dressing each in turn until the side walls are reached. Once the last panes are fitted the flashing can be reached more easily. Use non-setting mastic to seal the side walls to the house, and finish off by running a bead along the bottom of the side walls to seal them to the base.

It may be necessary to restore or replace internal fixtures and fittings, such as staging and shelves, and floor coverings. What you do about the former depends very much on their condition and how much time and trouble you are prepared to accept in order to save them – wholesale replacement might be more economical. As for the flooring, it may be possible to lift loose quarry tiles, slabs, ceramic tiles or mosaics, and re-lay them, although the last two items will involve more work because of their smallness. If the existing flooring is beyond repair, lift it and lay a new screed over a damp-proof membrane ready for a new floorcovering.

If the conservatory is a true period piece, you may wish to replace damaged components in a matching style. In timber this should not be too much of a problem – local wood carvers and turners should be able to reproduce the existing patterns, but for such work the price will be high. Cast-iron work, however, would be too expensive to copy, but you could experiment with casting

replicas in plastic resin, or you may be able to find similar items in local demoliton yards or tucked away in the corner of an architectural salvager's yard. Genuine ornamental work of the type used in Victorian conservatories can sometimes be found in such places and the thrill of the chase will encourage you to track down what you want.

Building a Wardian window

If there is insufficient space for a conservatory, you can still display plants to wonderful effect and gain some of the advantages of a conservatory on a smaller scale by creating what is known as a Wardian window. This is named after a Victorian botanist who devised a glass-sided case for displaying ferns and other moisture-loving plants; a Wardian window is simply a 'double-glazed' window with plants growing between the panes. It can be created in almost any window opening, provided the reveal is deep enough to contain a planting trough of reasonable size. The idea is particularly suited to bow windows and the small semi-circular or triangular oriel windows often found on stairs and landings. It is only necessary to place a planter on the sill and add another pane of glass on the inside to make what is a miniature greenhouse. The inner pane should, ideally, be mounted in a frame so it can be opened and closed easily – depending on the type of window it could be hinged or sliding. The principle is similar to secondary double-glazing, and it may be possible to use the plastic or metal frame members marketed for that purpose.

A slightly more adventurous alteration would be to replace the existing window frame with a custom-built display case. This should have a fixed pane on the outside (perhaps containing a small ventilator) and a hinged or sliding pane on the inside. The sides, top, and bottom of the opening could be lined with timber, and shelves fitted on adjustable shelf studs to allow smaller plants to be displayed in the top half of the window, leaving the bottom half free for larger plants in a planting trough at sill level.

Lastly, if you have large areas of floor-to-ceiling glazing you could create a spectacular effect by building a free-standing mobile unit rather like a glass-fronted shelving unit, mounting it on castors and wheeling it into a position where it will receive the most amount of sunlight. Taller species could be grown in a case of this size, making it a highly distinctive feature of a room – using it, perhaps, as a room divider in the evening when the sun has set.

A Victorian wrought-iron and glass case, or Wardian window, on the outside of a house. Fully enclosed when the sash window is down and supported by decorative brackets, it forms a miniature conservatory. The kind of plants used would depend on its aspect – this, with its palms and dracaenas, would have faced south.

Making the most of a splendid view over the garden, the owner of the study opposite has replaced the original window with a new, extended one, making more space for plants on its sill. To some extent it simulates the Wardian window above.

Heat, Ventilation and Light

The ideal temperature for an attached greenhouse or conservatory depends on its role. Is it to be mainly a place to relax in, or for small children to play in, right through the year? Do you see it as a cheerful extra room for sitting in – and for entertaining – during the warmer months only? Or will it have to serve double duty as a greenhouse, whether to produce pot plants during all seasons, for the spring propagation of annuals, or even as a hothouse for growing exotics regardless of outdoor temperatures?

While this emphasis on plant-growing needs particular thought, a conservatory used solely as living space requires special consideration as well. In the first case the emphasis is on creating an ideal environment for plants whereas in the second case human comfort becomes the objective.

Given an orientation that enjoys some sunshine, there is no doubt that conservatories score heavily over greenhouses in the all-important matter of heating. Free-standing greenhouses, which nowadays so often have glass to ground level on all four sides, are vulnerable to every chilling wind that blows and lose their accumulated day-time warmth very soon after nightfall. Maintaining an adequate temperature to grow a fairly wide range of pot plants can be costly indeed, while the inevitable fluctuations arising from changes in the outside temperature – most severe for plants placed close to the glass – make for uneven and uncertain results.

A conservatory or three-sided greenhouse gains by being sheltered from the wind on at least one side and having a smaller area of glass subject to drastic heat loss. This alone will reduce heating costs and make for more even temperatures. But the advantages do not stop there ...

Conservatories and heat storage

Whereas a greenhouse has virtually only its soil to store daytime warmth, a conservatory has at least one wall and a floor to serve as 'storage radiators'. Very often there is an additional end wall, and perhaps also a thigh-level wall beneath the glass. When constructed of a dense building material – bricks or blocks, not wood – these retain a significant amount of the sun's radiant warmth, which they emit gradually during the hours of darkness. Even in winter and overcast weather the effect is significant and it becomes progressively more marked during the spring propagation period as days lengthen and nights shorten.

This storage effect also offers something of a bonus in conservatories used mainly to provide living accommodation.

A large south-facing, double-glazed conservatory attached to a low-energy demonstration house, both of which have been designed to achieve minimum heating costs during the winter. Basically, warm air generated in the conservatory passes into the solar collector on the roof and is either blown into the house or directed through a heat pump to provide hot water, which is ducted into a storage tank in the house. The stored heat provides warm air for space heating during sunless weather. When solar heat is marginal a solid fuel stove provides heat through a back boiler. To prevent overheating in hot weather a series of flaps create a continuous flow of cool air over the collector's surface and there is a system of insulated louvres and panels in the conservatory to control winter losses and summer gains.

Proportionately less heat is needed during the evening, while the generally warmer and more stable atmosphere helps to prevent overnight condensation.

In a favourable situation it is possible to use a conservatory as a passive solar heat collector to supplement the household heating (see p. 114) and, in the U.S.A., such rooms receive tax credits as 'passive' solar heating units. When orientation and roof slope are appropriate, installing solar panels for home heating or to preheat domestic hot water can work well. Since in the Northern Hemisphere, solar panels are most efficient when facing true south and tilted to an angle of approximately 15° plus the latitude of the region, they are least noticed and most aesthetically acceptable on a roof of similar slope and orientation. When freestanding on a flat roof, however, the solar panels may become aesthetically undesirable, detracting from the appearance of the building.

The storage effect is much less marked in a north-facing conservatory receiving little or no direct sunshine. Even so, as explained earlier, such a conservatory does have it own possibilities and heat storage is not lost completely. Whatever the situation, bear in mind that a dark surface tends to absorb heat, a light surface to reflect it, so the common practice of painting the backing wall white may not be such a good idea, except on a south-facing wall.

The shape of the conservatory, too, plays a part. The simplest and commonest type of lean-to structure, with its longest side parallel with one of the house walls, provides the greatest amount of heat-storage area. In contrast, a conservatory that projects outwards from the house and covers only a small area of wall will cool down more rapidly in the evening. Heat loss is even more marked in a projecting conservatory exposed to cooling winds and in situations where a substantial part of the house wall is taken up by entrance doors.

Of course, even a south-facing conservatory will not always retain a great deal of daytime warmth after dark in winter. And even at midday it may be cold when the sky is overcast and the outdoor temperature low. Artificial heating is needed in any structure that is to be lived in between autumn and spring or that will house anything but the hardiest of plants.

Extending central heating

The obvious and easiest means is to extend an existing central heating system in order to supply one or more radiators in the

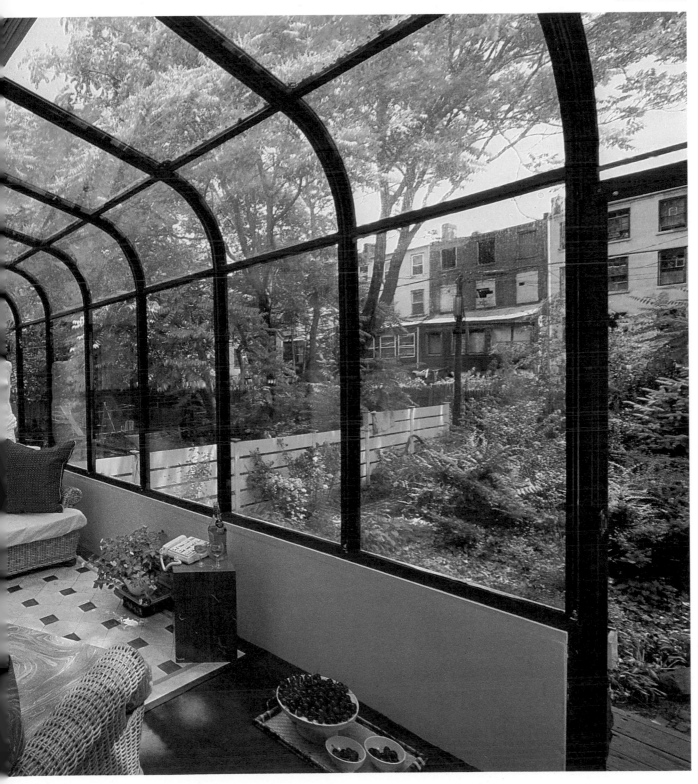

An elegant modular glassed-in living room, constructed of bronze-finish aluminium and fully double glazed to prevent heat loss. The long house wall aids heat storage and shading is provided by Roman blinds.

conservatory. The installation should not cost a great deal if the existing pipework comes fairly close to the conservatory wall, while operating costs will be much lower than if a separate system of, say, electric heaters is fitted.

There are possible snags, however, and you should in any case get expert local advice to ensure that the present heat source will cope with the extra area of radiators. The heating engineer who checks this will also advise on the size of radiators needed – often larger than for an equivalent-sized indoor room because of the heat loss through glass. If the glass is fitted with night-time insulating covers, the radiators may not need to be larger.

One of the snags is that the existing central heating may be controlled by a thermostat fitted at a carefully chosen point indoors. This will obviously not give very sensitive control for the conservatory – perhaps exposed to a chilly east wind. Also, there is probably a time clock that switches off the system at night, which may not be a problem if the conservatory is used solely as living space but is the opposite of what is needed where tender plants are grown.

Although of traditional shape, this conservatory – like the one illustrated on the previous page – is built on modular principles. It is double glazed, has automatic ventilation, internal roof blinds and many other modern features. However, sited end-on to the house wall, it is likely to cool more quickly.

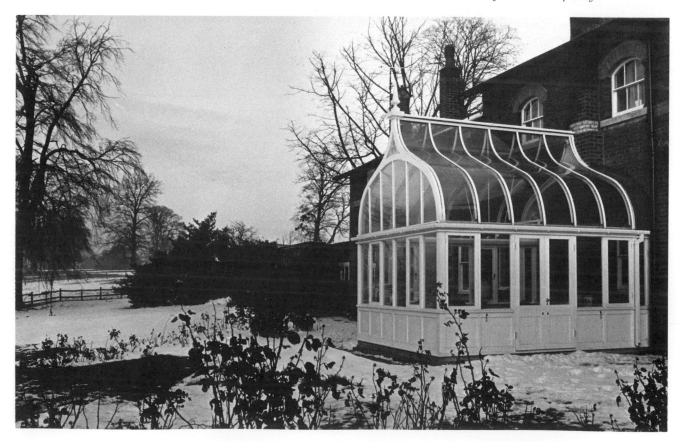

There are a number of ways of resolving both problems (solenoid valves will isolate radiators at night) but this again stresses the need for expert advice.

One relatively simple solution is to install a thermostatically-controlled fan heater that will cut in when the night-time temperature in the conservatory drops below a critical level. The latter will depend principally on what plants are being grown. What you should not do, however, is simply to leave open the entrance doors from the living room. This will cool down the house quite markedly, but without raising the temperature in the conservatory sufficiently to protect tender plants.

Left to his own devices, the plumber or heating engineer may position the new radiators against the house wall – the most convenient place from his point of view. But it may not be the ideal spot for any plants that you choose to grow. It really depends on whether the glass will extend to ground level or whether you plan to have a low wall along the front, perhaps with staging for pot plants and seed raising fixed level with the top. In the latter case, low-level radiators fastened against the outer wall and under the staging will be of greatest benefit to the plants and will hep to counteract the downward movement of air that results from the chilling effect of the glass.

However, if you have a glass-to-ground conservatory you will not want radiators placed just inside the transparent outer wall. In any case, you may choose to grow your plants elsewhere – standing them on the floor or perhaps hanging them from the rear wall – and this is surely a case where aesthetics may be allowed to win the day over efficiency.

The above assumes that you plan to fit hot-water baseboard radiators or ordinary panel radiators, as used elsewhere in the house. However, you will do better to choose the fan convector type, in which an electric fan distributes the warmed air throughout the conservatory. One or more radiators of this type will give much improved heat distribution and help to avoid the pockets of cold air that may otherwise remain away from the heat source. Probably the best position for installing a fan convector radiator in a rectangular conservatory is against one of the shorter walls, so that the warm air is blown across the longest stretch of glass. But this is not practicable in a large structure where two or more radiators are required. It is worth noting here that a small room air-conditioner – a sizal gas unit – produces enough *BTUs* to heat a 12 × 14ft (3½ × 4¼m) greenhouse.

These fan convectors are smaller than ordinary radiators, occupying less wall space and fitting in neatly where there might otherwise be a problem of arranging furniture. Usually, they are fastened to the wall at a fairly low level but there are also down-draught types for mounting above head level. The fan motor is audible but the sound will hardly be noticed after a short while. The fan can be switched on in the summer, when the heating is not in use, to improve air circulation throughout the conservatory.

Of course, it may be that you do not have central heating or that the existing system cannot be extended. Fortunately, there are a number of other options, while it may be noted once again that the plant-growing conservatory owner has a marked advantage over his greenhouse-owning neighbour. This is because he is saved the cost and probable disruption of laying outdoor extensions to the electricity and/or gas supplies – both jobs for professionals. So, indeed, is extending either of these services to the conservatory, but the distance will be minimal and there are no paths, drives or lawns to be dug up.

To heat the conservatory by some means other than extending the central heating you will have to choose between electricity, gas, solid fuel and paraffin (kerosene). Of these, electricity is certainly the most satisfactory, but also the most expensive to maintain, one major advantage being that it does not increase humidity and cause the heavy condensation that results from both gas and paraffin heaters. It lends itself to totally automatic control, is clean and fume-free and virtually 100 per cent efficient. Running costs are considerably higher than for other fuels but the difference has tended to decrease in recent years as gas prices have risen. Nonetheless electric heat is expensive.

Electric heaters

There are two main types of electrical appliances suitable for this purpose – tubular heaters and fan heaters. The former, which are slightly more expensive, provide a permanent installation which is quite easily fitted by an amateur. However, the extension wiring to the new supply point should be left to a professional.

Tubular heaters are simply electric heating elements encased in protective metal tubing. They are rated at 60 or 80 watts per foot (30cm) run. The tubes are secured horizontally near the foot of the wall in mounting brackets, either singly or in banks, and may be fitted with wire guards – essential if children will be in the area.

Tubular heaters respond rapidly when switched on and give an even distribution of warmth if correctly sited. They are ideal for thermostatic control – essential for economic running – and may, in addition, be controlled by a time switch for daytime use only if the conservatory is not to house tender plants. Alternatively, if the household central heating warms the conservatory by day, the switch can bring in the heaters at night to protect such plants.

Where plants are to be grown, inevitably resulting in more humid conditions, it is important to fit tubular heaters designed specifically for use in greenhouses and conservatories. These have aluminium covers, which resist corrosion indefinitely. When fitting a bank of heaters – generally two, three or four deep – the lowest should be about 9in (23cm) clear of the floor. If you fit a shelf or staging above the heaters, leave a space of about 6in (15cm) between this and the wall so that the flow of air is not interrupted. Spread the tubes as widely as possible, rather than having a multi-tube bank in just one part of the conservatory. This, as you would expect, gives more even heat distribution through the conservatory.

A fan heater is the main alternative, a familiar household appliance which has only to be plugged in and can also be used to concentrate heat on a particular area. Many have built-in thermostats, though a fan heater does not always maintain a constant level of warmth throughout a room. Also, some people object to its low background hum. Running costs are virtually the same as for tubular heaters but the latter, being fixed installations with no moving parts, are even less likely to develop faults.

Once again, if plant-growing is a significant activity – resulting in more humid or even damp conditions – choose a fan heater designed for greenhouse use. For preference, go for a model that can be switched to give different levels of heat – usually 1kW, 2kW or 3kW. It is also an advantage if the fan can be run without any of the heating elements being switched on, providing a cooling flow of air during warm weather in summer.

There is evidence that the steady movement of air from a fan heater promotes healthier plant growth, presumably because it prevents the development of moulds and fungi which thrive in a warm, stagnant atmosphere. The other advantage of a fan heater is its almost immediate effect on temperature. To obtain full advantage from this rapid response, buy a heater with a sensitive and reliable thermostat, or control it with an independent thermostat placed elsewhere in the conservatory.

As a rule, the thermostat controls only the heating element. The motor and fan keep running all the time the appliance is switched on which, of course, does ensure continuous air circulation. If you are concerned about economy, buy a heater with a thermostat that controls both heater and fan.

Unless you wish to concentrate warmth in a particular spot, position the fan heater at one end of the conservatory so that the current of warm air flows along its length. If you find that one part of the building tends to get warmer than others, position plants accordingly.

Electric underfloor heating is, if your conservatory has yet to be built, another option. Operated by cables laid directly in the concrete base, it provides a remarkably even level of warmth throughout the whole structure and, of course, takes up no space at all in the conservatory itself. However, it does respond rather slowly to thermostatic control and running costs may prove unacceptably high. If it does appeal to you (after getting a *realistic* estimate of these costs) be sure to get expert advice on installation.

Night storage heaters, running on a lower utility rate in certain locations, might be considered if the conservatory is for living space only. But they are rather inflexible for a structure that can gain so much warmth from the sun, while there are periods of reduced heat output that may not match with the needs of plants.

Although not a means of space heating, electric soil-warming cables should be mentioned here because they will provide localized heat for plant propagation and early growth in conservatories where the overall temperature is on the low side or subject to fluctuations. Even so, they will not entirely compensate for a chilly environment and it is as well to make the propagation bed inside a wooden frame which can be covered with glass or plastic to retain as much warmth as possible. The whole unit can be placed on staging or on the conservatory floor.

Heating by gas

Reverting to overall space heating, gas is cheaper in terms of operating costs when compared with electricity. Throughout the United States utility rates vary, depending on several factors – proximity to power plants being one. In general the cost of electricity per *BTU* of heat is greater than oil or natural gas. Capital outlay for the heater will be roughly comparable with that for an electric fan heater, though the work involved with connections to the existing gas supply may be more extensive than running an extra length of electric cable.

It is also possible to burn propane gas, supplied in cylinders, instead of piped gas. Installation involves no more than connecting the supply pipe from the cylinder to the heater, but propane costs a good deal more than mains gas.

A major snag with both types of gas, however, is the large amount of water vapour given off during combustion. In the absence of a flue this is released into the conservatory, leading to condensation, unless the unit is vented to the outside.

If gas heating does appeal, choose a model with an effective thermostat. The most sensitive are electric, placed at some distance from the heater. Electricity consumption is very small, although there will be a little extra installation work.

However, the finer points of gas heaters may not be all that relevant. Propane offers no decisive advantages over electricity, while householders with a supply of piped gas will very often already have central heating – which in many cases can be extended to heat the conservatory. If this proves impracticable, electric heaters are generally to be preferred to unflued gas-fired appliances. Manufacturers make much of the benefits for plant growth of the enrichment of the atmosphere by the carbon dioxide that comes from gas heating, but this, compared with a commercial glasshouse, is of minimal importance in the average domestic conservatory.

Paraffin or kerosene heaters

The same criticism can be made of paraffin heaters – another possible form of heating for small conservatories. Condensation is certain to be heavy, though this must be balanced against moderate running costs and ease of installation. The 'blue flame' type of heater burns with little or no smell, which cannot be said of yellow-flame heaters.

However, paraffin heating is not really ideal for a living-space conservatory. Heat distribution is poor and a single heater would prove inadequate for any but the smallest of structures. Safety is another consideration and the appliance should be screwed or bolted to the floor.

If paraffin heaters do have a part to play it is mainly as a standby for emergency or supplementary use in severe weather or as an additional heat source to help raise plants in spring. The trouble is that some degree of ventilation is needed to combat condensation if either paraffin or gas heaters are used, thus reducing the effectiveness of either system.

Hot-water systems

Solid-fuel heaters, circulating hot water through pipes, used to be the principal means of warming conservatories and greenhouses.

They are relatively uncommon now but it is still possible to buy small boilers designed especially for the purpose. The appliance stands outside one end of the conservatory, with the flow and return pipes – usually 4in (10cm) in diameter – extending along one or more walls.

Capital outlay is higher than for other heating systems. Running costs are roughly comparable with paraffin. The principal advantages are even heat distribution and the fact that no water vapour is emitted. The principal disadvantage is the fairly frequent attention needed by the fire, while you may not care for the look of a boiler attached rather prominently to part of your living space.

Mainly because of the work involved, solid fuel boilers have lost much of their former appeal. Also, they can be a tie if you wish to spend a weekend away from home. Both problems are solved by fitting, instead, a paraffin-fired boiler. This, too, heats a system of hot-water pipes mounted round the walls, but with the boiler positioned inside the conservatory. If you prefer to have it outside, a protective cover must be built around it.

Combustion gases are taken up through a flue, so there is no condensation problem as with free-standing paraffin heaters. A separate fuel tank connected to the boiler will keep the burner supplied for long periods. Even so, heaters of this type are strictly for conservatories where the emphasis is on plant-growing. They are unsuitable for small structures intended mainly to increase living space.

Electrical installation

The advantages of electric heating have been mentioned (but remember the disadvantage if power failures are likely in your area), and this form of power will also be needed for lighting and possibly to assist ventilation.

If the planned use of the garden room or conservatory is simply to be an additional living room, then standard fittings, power sockets and switches may be used. However, as already suggested, plant-growing on any scale inevitably gives rise to increased humidity, while in some conservatories there will be a watering programme comparable to that in a greenhouse. Under these conditions it is necessary to use fittings designed specifically for such situations and for the wiring to be designed accordingly. There are special regulations covering this and you must make it clear to a qualified electrician just what sort of usage you have in mind.

This single-glazed, lean-to plant house, built in 1901, is heated during the winter by hot-water pipes from the house central-heating system. Being frost free, a wide range of plants can be grown.

101

For a conservatory used largely for plant-growing, all appliances should, ideally, be supplied from a greenhouse-style control panel. Connected to the incoming cable, it includes an overall isolating switch together with individually-switched socket outlets, and fused switches for lighting or tubular heater circuits. All are permanently wired, so that the only connection needed is to the mains supply. Such panels come complete with mounting brackets for fitting, if required, to the glazing bars.

The circuit must be protected by a residual current device (RCD), also known as an earth leakage circuit breaker. This is an extremely valuable safety aid, for it turns off the current automatically in a fraction of a second should a short occur. Thus even a mains-voltage shock is unlikely to do much harm.

In an ordinary living-room-style conservatory it will be up to you, of course, to decide how many light fittings and power sockets you are likely to need and where they should be placed, which is why you need to decide on heating methods before putting the work in hand. Even so, it is not always easy to know exactly how you will use the building before you start to live in it, so err on the generous side when specifying power points. One or two extra will cost very little at that stage but would be a major expense and cause upheaval if added later. With this in mind, fit twin sockets instead of single outlets so that more than one appliance can be powered simultaneously in the same area of the conservatory – a fan heater and a standard lamp, for instance.

If you are really confident about the positioning of electrical aids, position sockets accordingly to suit any appliance that will be well clear of the floor. Wiring for a bench-level propagator or soil-warmed bed, or a high-level fan, will be less obtrusive if the outlet is positioned as close to the appliance as possible.

Humidity and condensation

One of the attractions of a double-glazed conservatory is that, for practical purposes, condensation is eliminated. However, double-glazing adds at least a third to the initial outlay, and frequently causes problems with the result that the majority of new structures in Britain and the U.S.A. are still single-glazed.

Fortunately, condensation should not prove to be a substantial problem even in single-glazed buildings unless a considerable number of plants are grown. In this case, the presence of damp soil or compost, along with transpiration from the plants, is bound to increase humidity. This is no problem at all during the warmer months, while ventilation is liberal, but it can result in streaming glass during the colder part of the year when both indoor and outdoor temperatures are lower and ventilation minimal. However, the extra humidity will bring welcome relief to dry throats.

For effective control of excess condensation it is as well to understand what causes it. It may be helpful to think of the air in the conservatory as a sponge, which can take up only so much moisture until a stage is reached when any excess is shed. Warm air has a greater moisture-holding capacity than does cold, so a well-heated building will suffer less from condensation than one with poor heating or none at all. Also, a well-insulated building will have less condensation than a poorly insulated one.

Even so, the air will shed some of its moisture the moment it cools, as witness the beads of moisture that form on a glass of iced water, which cools the air immediately adjacent to it. Exactly the same thing happens with window glass, where the air outside cools first the glass and then the air indoors that touches it. The 'sponge' loses some of its capacity and moisture is shed.

Air in a 'living-room' conservatory is seldom saturated to this extent, partly because there are likely to be only a few plants and also because generous heating will have made the air absorbent. Only if an unflued gas or paraffin heater is installed is there likely to be a serious problem.

The twin answers to condensation on any scale – apart from removing the source of moisture – are ventilation and warmth. Ventilation provides a change of air, carrying away excess moisture. Warmth increases the moisture-carrying capacity of the air and is also needed to compensate for the cooling effect of the ventilation.

Condensation may still occur even in a double-glazed conservatory, not on the glass but on a cold, exterior wall should this be a feature of the design. Insulating the wall can solve this problem. One way to do this may be to cover the wall with a sheet of expanded polystyrene, then to paper over it. However, before doing this a careful check of the local fire regulations should be made for this material can constitute an unacceptable fire hazard.

Condensation may even be evident on carpeting, due to a cold sub-floor. Short of major structural work, the most practical answers are to use a warmer floor covering and to pay extra attention to heating and ventilation, especially during cold spells.

Do not be disturbed if your newly-erected conservatory sheds heavy condensation. This is quite normal while the concrete floor screed dries out. This may go on for several weeks, depending on weather conditions, and it is important that the floor covering

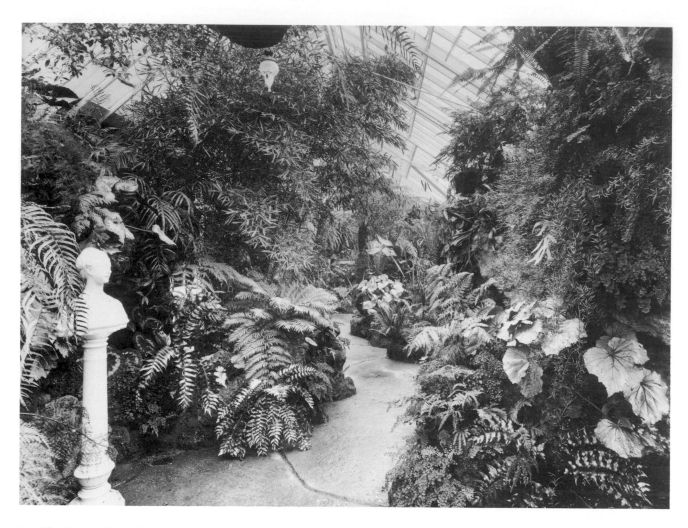

itself – be it tiles, sheet plastic or carpet – should not be laid until the screed is quite dry. On average, a week should be allowed for each ¼in (6mm) of thickness. As most screeds are about 2in (5cm) thick, this means a full two months.

Although an excessively moist atmosphere, leading to condensation, is a fairly common situation, the very opposite may cause difficulties for the many conservatory owners who enjoy growing a variety of house plants. For it is a fact that some of these plants *need* a humid atmosphere and are unhappy in the warm, dry conditions found in most modern living rooms. There are also some house plants whose need for humidity increases with the temperature, a combination of high temperature and low humidity being, at worst, fatal.

The easiest way to increase humidity is to invest in an ordinary household humidifier. There are several makes, and their special

Built in 1903, this large private conservatory was devoted almost entirely to growing varieties of ferns that require warmth and humidity. It would have been heated by hot-water pipes running from a solid-fuel boiler.

advantage is that they do away with, or certainly reduce, the need for misting with a sprayer – a rather messy business in the average living room.

For just a handful of small plants, hardly justifying a humidifier, the answer is to stand them on a tray filled with damp gravel. Alternatively, stand each pot in a larger one, filling the space with damp peat. In both cases, the moisture-holding medium will need regular replenishment.

Ventilation

We have seen that ventilation is needed to combat a stagnant, humid atmosphere during the colder months. It is even more vital once winter is over if the conservatory is not to become an oven. It takes only a very short time on a summer's morning for the temperature to rise quite dramatically if there is not an efficient form of ventilation.

All conservatories are supplied with opening sky lights or roof vents, in the walls as well as in the roof. If the conservatory is built in front of a living room, and encloses that room's windows, the ventilation area in the conservatory must comply with the local building regulations. Because these regulations vary, it is impossible to give a precise figure. One code, for example, states that it must be equal to at least one-twentieth of the floor area of the two rooms put together. By no means will all this ventilation area be used for much of the time, but there will inevitably be days when you will welcome all the air movement you can get.

The problem, such as it is, concerns the control of these ventilators. In most cases they will be hinged roof vents, with stays for securing them in either the open or shut position. Or they may take the form of louvres. Both are adequate when there is someone around to deal with them, though the rapid heat gain in a conservatory means that more attention is needed than in a normal living room. But there is a difficulty at times when the conservatory is unoccupied, whether for just a day or during a holiday. If left closed, the inside temperature may soar and kill the plants. If left open, the inside may become chilly and damp, perhaps even with rain driving in. What is needed is an automatic system that responds almost instantly to weather changes, regardless of whether or not the house is occupied.

There are two possibilities – automatic, non-electric vent-openers, introduced primarily for greenhouses, or a thermostatically-controlled extractor fan to act in place of the vents. Both have their advantages and disadvantages.

The air-flow pattern in a typical well-ventilated lean-to conservatory. Warm air, generated by the heat of the sun, will rise by convection to leave through the multiple roof vents. In wet weather an extractor fan, which should be situated in the side facing away from the prevailing wind, can be used. The heated air is replaced by cool air drawn in through the low level louvre vents in the front and the hinged side vent.

Automatic vent-openers, which are operated by the expansion or contraction of a heat-sensitive substance inside a cylinder, are relatively inexpensive, cost nothing to run, are easy to fit, need no electricity supply and are silent in operation. They can be fitted to as many roof vents as you wish and can be relied upon to open or close without further attention. There are also models for controlling louvred ventilators.

There are one or two drawbacks, however. In a south-facing conservatory you may feel the need for a positive form of ventilation, as opposed to the passive opening of roof vents. But even more important is the simple fact that these openers, designed primarily for greenhouse use, are simply not powerful enough to open the much heavier roof vents fitted to some makes of conservatories. Those of one manufacturer, for example, weigh 24lbs (11kg) each, which is far in excess of what they are designed to tackle.

Do not despair, however. The construction and specification of roof vents varies enormously, many being no heavier than those of a free-standing greenhouse. The answer is to check with the appliance manufacturer whether or not his product will suit the type of conservatory you have in mind.

Two systems of ventilation for lean-to sun lounges: on the left, an automatic roof vent controlled by a thermostat that can be set to a pre-determined temperature; above, a multi-bladed louvre window in a side wall.

The alternative, an electric exhaust fan, does have distinct advantages, in spite of its substantially higher price. Provided you fit one that is large enough it will have an almost immediate effect on temperature and can be left to operate while you are on holiday. Similarly, it will clear a humid, stagnant atmosphere in a much shorter time than this takes by hinged lights.

Thermostatic control is essential for maximum benefit. The fan can be set in one of the side walls (glass or brick) or, if you prefer, you can buy a model for fitting in the roof. Automatic shutters can be fitted as a precaution against back-draughts, or in some cases they are integral with the fan. Special controllers are available to vary the direction of air-flow and to provide variable speeds.

Leading makers publish a simple formula in their sales literature to help customers choose the correct size of fan. This is based on the volume of the room (length x breadth x height) and the number of air changes needed per hour. They offer no specific advice on conservatories, but it would be wise to go for rather more than the three air changes per hour advised for living rooms. The relatively sudden temperature fluctuations in a conservatory call for a more powerful and immediate means of ventilation control.

If you do not have an exhaust fan, and possibly even if you *do* have one, a ceiling fan can also add to the comfort of a conservatory. Though not removing overheated air, it does prevent a stagnant atmosphere and makes windows and ventilators that much more effective. The improvement is marked on a sultry summer's day.

When installing such a fan it should be set so that the blades are at least 18in (90cm) from any solid surface, otherwise the free movement of air will be affected. In most cases the fan can be set to move the air either upwards or downwards, so it is worth experimenting to see which has the better effect.

Shading

Ventilation alone is insufficient to cool a conservatory during hot summer weather. Some form of shading is essential – unless it faces north – and this will also reduce glare. There are a number of possibilities.

At the lower end of the scale are brush-on preparations for applying to the outside of the glass. They are unaffected by rain but are easily brushed off at the end of the season. These products are intended primarily for greenhouses and, being opaque, they are unsuitable for general use on conservatories. However, a liquid shading material of this sort might be used for a small end wall should this be the only one exposed to direct sunlight. Economy is the chief advantage.

Of much greater appeal to most conservatory owners are adjustable blinds of one sort or another, which can be raised or lowered from the outside without fuss to suit the conditions of the moment. There are a good many makes and types, offering a choice of materials and also the option of fitting the blinds inside or outside the glass, though the latter is more common.

Reeded or slatted types on the outside are the most efficient, for they keep the glass itself cool and, because they rest on top of the glazing bars or on specially-fitted metal rails, there is a free flow of air between blinds and glass. However, many conservatory owners feel that this advantage is outweighed by their rather cumbersome appearance and by their exposure to wind and weather. It is, of course, necessary to go outdoors to make even a simple adjustment.

Indoor roller blinds, though a little less effective, are a good deal more convenient and do not detract from the conservatory's appearance. The rollers are spring-loaded, so that the blinds roll up tightly and effortlessly when not in use. It is worth noting that

A city rooftop lean-to conservatory. In a sunny site the necessary shading is provided by manually operated slatted blinds on the exterior.

fabric roller blinds mounted inside a conservatory help to reduce heat loss if they are pulled down on cold nights in winter. This is true, to an extent, of outdoor slatted blinds, but the effect is less marked. Indoor blinds can be tailored to fit shaped end walls, but outdoor blinds are made only for covering roofs and sides.

A wide variety of fabrics is used for indoor blinds, some natural and others synthetic. The latter have the advantage of being moisture-resistant. Colours are equally variable, the best choice here being something light and unobstrusive. Pale green is particularly restful to the eyes.

With outdoor blinds, too, a decision will have to be made between natural materials, such as slatted cedar, or synthetic products, which include extruded plastic reeds and mats of woven polyethylene. The former have a certain elegance but the life expectancy of both sorts will depend on how they are handled and on the degree of exposure of the site.

Lighting

Conventional living-room lighting will serve, if this is to be the main function of the conservatory. However, many owners like to introduce a hint of garden-style fittings into their lighting arrangements, often opting for coach-style lamps made of cast metal. A wide range of such fittings will be found at specialist shops and also at many department stores.

It must be admitted, however, that these may not be adequate as the only means of lighting for reading or any form of close work. With this in mind, a lighting track is often fitted along the ridge, with spot lamps that can be angled and moved. With separate switching, the spots can be left off at times when only general illumination is needed. An alternative would be one or two small standard lamps with adjustable heads for directing the light where required.

In addition to functional lighting, it is worth considering additional illumination purely for decorative purposes. In particular, bearing in mind the garden connotations of a conservatory, a low-level light directed upwards to display one or more plants looks particularly effective.

Returning to functional lighting, but of a quite different type, keen plant growers should consider installing one or more of the special lamps developed to promote plant growth during the winter and early spring when natural-light levels are low. It is often thought that warmth, nourishment, and moisture are all that plants need, but without abundant light the vital process of

Internal Roman roof blinds of a gauzy fabric give partial shading. Because only a little light is obstructed they cast a gentle diffuse shade.

photosynthesis will be hampered. (This provides plants with energy by converting carbon dioxide in the atmosphere, and hydrogen in water, into nourishing sugars.)

The subject is fairly complex and those interested in taking it further should refer to a specialist book which covers it in detail. It suffices to say here that it is not simply a matter of placing plants close to ordinary domestic lamps. Particular kinds are needed – either 'warm white' fluorescent tubes or mercury-vapour high-intensity discharge lamps. If this sounds rather formidable, the latter are actually quite small and unobstrusive. They have a marked effect on plant growth – particularly that of seedlings and young plants – making it possible virtually to ignore the seasons within the illuminated area. The lamps are readily available, but installation should be left to an electrician.

Watering

A small watering can and, perhaps, a one-quart (1-litre) trigger-type sprayer, will suffice for house plants kept in a conservatory used principally as a living room. But the possibilities are broader if plant-growing is a major function. It is worth giving the matter some thought, for traditional greenhouse methods, including watering with a hose, may not be acceptable in a building with direct access to the house. You will probably wish to keep the floor as clean and dry as possible so that water and mess do not get trodden indoors.

Other than using the time-consuming watering can, the most suitable methods in a conservatory are either trickle or capillary watering. The former employs small-bore tubes, with tee connectors to take branches to the pots and other containers. A drip nozzle is fitted to the end of each branch.

Capillary watering depends on the comparatively dry compost in pots and trays drawing up water from a base which is kept permanently damp.

Day-to-day watering apart, a major advantage of both systems is that they can be designed to function automatically – a particular boon during a holiday and also a great time-saver throughout the growing season. However, the length of time that they will function unattended depends on whether the system is fed directly from the mains or from a reservoir – often a sturdy plastic bag sold specially for the purpose – which itself needs refilling at intervals. Yet, even with a bag reservoir you will find it easier to recruit a neighbour to attend to this while you are away than to ask for daily hand-watering.

RESERVOIR

WATER
SUPPLY

TEE CONNECTORS

WATER
SUPPLY

DRIP
NOZZLE

'WICK'

WATER
RESERVOIR

CAPILLARY
MATTING

PLASTIC
SHEETING

Trickle watering is particularly suitable for supplying fairly large pots, tubs, growing bags and the like. It is unsuitable for watering seed trays or individual small pots but can be used as one means of keeping capillary matting moist – the absorbent material generally used as a base for capillary watering systems. Unfortunately, precise control of the outlets is not always as easy or positive as the makers may claim. It would be unwise to use a drip-watering system in a conservatory where excessive output, perhaps leading to minor flooding, might cause damage.

This problem should not occur with a correctly-installed capillary system. The essentials are a level bench or staging, covered first with sheet plastic and then with capillary matting. If cut a little longer than the bench, one end can be turned over into a trough or similar reservoir to keep the matting supplied continuously. Note, however, that the maximum 'lift' of the matting is 2in (5cm). Soak the matting thoroughly with a can of water before placing pots on it.

Providing the compost in containers is actually touching the matting, as much water will be drawn up as is needed to keep the compost continually moist. Most plants thrive on this treatment, though a few, including pelargoniums (geraniums), object to

The problem of keeping plants watered while you are on holiday without imposing on neighbours can, to a certain extent, be overcome. Above left: the trickle system works by gravity. A reservoir of water, in this case a plastic bag, is joined to small-bore tubes by tee connectors, and each tube end has a drip nozzle for controlling the water flow. Above: the capillary system is quite different. The matting, available from retail sources, is separated from the bench by plastic sheeting and its ends turned down into the water reservoirs. The matting acts as a large sponge, drawing up water from the reservoirs and, provided it is in contact with the compost, into the pots (left-hand pot). For thicker containers it will be necessary to make a 'wick' from the matting material to ensure proper contact (right-hand pot).

such damp conditions. Thin plastic pots are best, as the compost around the bottom hole touches the matting. If thicker, earthenware pots are used, cut a short 'wick' from the matting and insert half of this through the hole to ensure continuous contact. Poke the protruding end through a slit cut in the matting.

The Conservatory as a Passive Solar Space

The traditional conservatory has some of the features essential for a passive solar space. A passive solar conservatory or sunspace, however, is especially designed to use the natural elements for most of its heating and cooling needs.

The glass

The first and most important factor is orientation. Because in the Northern Hemisphere, true south receives the most sun during the winter months, a passive solar space functions best when facing true south but not more than 30° east or west of true south. With this restriction, the sun penetrates deep into the space in winter and may be easier to control during the summer months when it is high in the sky. In fact, on a clear winter day, a general southern exposure assures sunshine in the conservatory from about 9.00 a.m. to 3.00 p.m., resulting in significant heat gain.

When adding a sunspace to an existing building, its south facade is clearly the most appropriate yet it may not always be suitable to receive the new room. Property restrictions, adjoining buildings, and existing spatial layout can stand in the way of the solar extension. Even when the south portion of the building is available for a sunspace addition, the surrounding structures and trees or terrain may cause excessive shading. In a densely populated area, future construction that blocks the sun may also be a problem. In many instances, however, with a clear access to the south, a building is suitable for a solar conservatory or sunspace addition.

As always, the architectural style of the conservatory is up to the designer, but the type of glazing selected and its placement should follow some general rules. Except in a mild climate, double glazing, or thermal windows are preferred over the traditional single glazing to reduce heat loss and drafts. To maximize efficiency further, most window openings should be placed on the south-facing wall, leaving the two end walls opaque and well insulated. With a solid roof, south-facing clerestory

RADIANT
SOLAR
ENERGY

FAN — WARM AIR

THERMAL ENERGY — FREE HEAT

COOL AIR — AIR VENT

The warm air in a conservatory produced by the heating effect of solar energy can be transferred to the adjoining room. Opening the connecting door will allow the warm air to enter the house by means of convection, but a simple thermostatically controlled fan installed high up, and an air vent positioned near the floor level will regulate the transfer of heat more efficiently.

windows are excellent in providing additional solar heat and light. When a glass roof is desired, a steep south-facing slope assures efficient wintertime solar penetration while reflecting the direct rays of the hot summer sun. Nevertheless, an all glass roof is often a problem, admitting too much sun in the summer and causing great heat loss in the winter. For this reason, the designer may select smaller overhead glazing in the form of roof vents that are operable, and can be equipped with various shading and insulating devices.

Thermal mass

In a sunspace, the heat storage effect of a traditional conservatory is maximized by careful design.

Thermal mass or heat storage materials have the capacity to soak in heat from solar radiation during the day and slowly release it after the sun sets. Mass can be part of the structure in the form of brick or masonry walls, or a concrete slab floor with quarry tiles, slate, or other masonry flooring. When the space has no masonry materials for heat storage, water can function as the storage element. Contained in 55 gallon (208 litre) drums, large plastic tubes or smaller units, water exposed to sunlight stores about five times as much heat as an equal weight of masonry. With both water and masonry, the colour of the mass determines how much of the sunlight is absorbed as heat. While black has the highest solar absorptivity, other dark colours such as brown and deep red are nearly as efficient.

When the thermal mass is entirely indoors, as with containers of water or an interior wall between the sunspace and other living spaces, it functions well in its cycle to absorb and release solar heat. When, however, the thermal storage is an exterior wall or a slab on grade (a floor resting directly on the earth), it should be well insulated on its exterior side. In this way when the mass releases its stored heat, most of the thermal energy radiates toward the interior spaces rather than to the outside.

The location of the heat-storage mass determines its effectiveness. The best use of a heat-storage material results when it receives direct sunlight for a considerable time. Achieving this is not a problem in a south-facing conservatory attached to an existing building along its length. When the sunspace extends away from, rather than along the south face of the existing building, sunlight may not reach certain inside surfaces.

The quantity of mass necessary for a good thermal balance depends on a region's climate and the amount of sunshine it receives in the wintertime. Using a floor as thermal storage, a 6-8in (15-20cm) concrete slab functions well. A solid masonry wall of 8-12in (20-30cm) between the sunspace and adjoining spaces is also a good choice. Since this type of wall gives off its stored heat toward adjoining spaces as well as the sunspace, it is especially useful in sunny temperate climates where the amount of heat collected by the sunspace on a clear day exceeds its own heating requirements.

With water thermal storage, using about 8 gallons of water for each square foot (325 litres per square metre) of south facing glass is usually sufficient. Some of the various containers now manufactured for this purpose can be permanently installed while smaller units are easily stacked up in a desired part of the room. Most often, containers are sealed to prevent leakage, and water is chemically treated to impede the growth of algae. Containers are generally black but can sometimes be painted a desired dark colour.

Flexible insulation

The same glass surfaces that admit the sunshine during the day in a sunspace become the chief source of heat loss at night, chilling individuals within. While well-sealed double-glazed window units help minimize these adverse influences, insulating window covers work best.

The increasing demand for energy-efficient designs has prompted manufacturers in Europe and the United States to respond with a number of energy-related products. Among these are a large selection of insulating window treatments. Good sealing, with a high thermal resistance, new shutters, blinds and curtains offer up to ten times the insulating value of double glazing.

The most critical glass area to insulate is overhead glazing.

Pull-down thermal blinds, or panels that fit snugly into roof vents work as shading in the summer and insulation on cold winter nights. An even wider variety of devices is available for vertical glazing, which is more easily fitted. The cost and effectiveness of window treatments vary – it is worth spending a little time researching into the pros and cons of the various treatments before making a final decision.

How much heat is gained?

The amount of heat gained by a sunspace depends on a number of factors. The climate of the region and the percentage of available solar radiation are major considerations. Generally, however, the area of glass facing the south determines how much solar heat is captured on a sunny day.

In many cases, the trapped solar energy is just enough to heat the space during the day and moderate its temperature at night, but sometimes more than enough heat may be captured. In those cases, heat can be transferred to and utilized by other, non-solar spaces within the building, thereby cutting heating costs. There are several ways to accomplish this.

The easiest is to transfer the heat passively through a masonry wall between the sunroom and adjoining spaces. This type of thermal wall works best when several rooms adjoin the sunspace. In double tier sunspace design, both floors can benefit from the stored solar energy.

When a floor slab or water containers are used for thermal storage, other methods can be employed to distribute heat. Sometimes, large doors, opened between the sunroom and other spaces, are sufficient for this. Often, though, not enough air flow takes place. To assure proper heat distribution, small openings or vents, equipped with dampers, at the top and bottom of the wall between the sunroom and other spaces, will encourage cool air to flow along the floor into the sunroom. The cool air, warmed by the sun, rises and circulates back into the adjoining rooms through the top vents. This air motion usually occurs by natural gravity convection but can be increased by mechanically ducting air to various parts of the house.

There are periods when a sunspace loses heat and becomes an energy drain on the house. This can occur during prolonged cloudiness or extremely cold and windy conditions. It is best to close off the space during these periods of severe weather. Nevertheless, to provide flexibility, a separately controlled heating system is often preferred. This supplementary heating system

This large American glass extension provides cover for a swimming pool. Completely double glazed and with adequate controls, full advantage is taken of its potential as a passive solar space.

can moderate night temperatures and provide a comfortable environment in the sunspace for use during the most adverse weather conditions.

Living with the sun

When conservatories first became popular for private use they were considered a status symbol, a luxury. Even today, the sunspace or solar conservatory addition to a house is looked upon as a special bonus to indoor living. In winter, it extends the interior space to the outside, yet offers shelter. In the summer, shaded and opened up, it encourages a maximum of outside airflow through it.

Sunspace living does have an impact on lifestyles. Individuals become aware of seasonal changes in the sun's position in the sky, arranging furniture and carpeting to avoid shading the heat-storage mass, and making a diligent effort to replace window insulators every night in winter and draw the shades and open vents in summer, for maximum comfort. Along with all this comes the realization of the cycles of nature: from day to night, from season to season. Thus, instead of seeking to keep the sunspace environment uniform, it is allowed to fluctuate in tune with the natural elements. However, because of this flexibility, the true sunspace may not be ideal for growing delicate plants. It is more an environment for semi-hardy plants and people who can enjoy it as a live-in solar collector.

Furnishings and Fittings

Fitting out a conservatory, greenhouse, garden room or any glass-enclosed extension needs just as much care and attention as any other form of interior decoration. These rooms should have style, and blend in naturally with the general theme of the house; in most cases there are almost as many ways of decorating and furnishing these garden rooms as for other rooms in the home.

Style and mood

First of all decide on the impression you want to create and the mood you wish to set. Colour will help you to achieve the right atmosphere, and the type of decoration, furniture and fabrics – including their surface design and texture – together with the flooring and window treatment, to give the room a personality and style.

Be guided by the architectural form of the building, be it romantically Regency, vigorously Victorian, elegantly Edwardian, or streamlined; whichever you choose, try to echo this flavour when you decide on decorations and furnishings. If it is a bland, non-architectural style room you will need to give it some character, so decide on a definite style and follow it through with the appropriate decorations, furniture and furnishings.

In many cases, the garden room or conservatory leads off from another room in the house, or from the end of the hall, and is the most pleasant and attractive way into the garden (if you're lucky enough to have one). It may be used as a living room, summer sitting room, dining room, or as a playroom and family room, alternatively it may simply be a traditional garden room, filled with plants.

But whatever the function, try to link it visually with the rest of the house or apartment, either by colour or your choice of pattern and design – or both. And try to echo some of the conservatory atmosphere in the room from which it leads. Lack of light may be a problem, and if this is the case, try to keep connecting space as bright and reflective as possible. Mirrors can help a lot, so can shiny surfaces, reflective foils and gloss paintwork, but remember, do not paint a brick or stone supporting wall white if you want to conserve heat.

The furniture for all kinds of garden room needs to look as good outside as in. The ideal choice is the indoor/outdoor variety, which can be used on the patio and in the garden during the summer. Many garden centres or garden furniture departments have a wide range of styles and prices, and are the best places to start looking.

Colour

The colour scheme will depend to some extent on the function of the room. If it is to be filled with plants, choose natural colours to enhance them, for example, greens, browns and earth tones, with a few bright contrasts as accessories. Avoid over-patterned floral fabrics, especially chintz, in this type of room.

In a more modern setting, use the bright primary colours for a stimulating effect, or if the space needs brightening, choose the sugared-almond range of pastels. The golden rules of colour scheming are the same for conservatories and garden rooms as for other rooms – use cool colours (blues, greens, lilacs, purples and greys) for a bright, sunny room – to tone them down. Choose the warmer ones (reds, yellow, orange, pink, peach, terracotta, browns) for cooler rooms which need warming up. Add a sharp touch of contrasting colour to a cool scheme, to bring it to life – this can also be done by means of accessories and plants.

In a small room use paler colours and simple patterns and textures, and select cooler colours, if you want to create an illusion of space. In a large room, use bright colours, or strong ones, and big, bold designs to make it seem smaller – more cosy and intimate.

Floorings

Because of needed humidity, plant watering and various potting and greenhouse activities, most conservatories and garden rooms need a completely washable and waterproof flooring. The majority of these tend to be fairly hard and unyielding underfoot, so if you want to use the space as an extension to the living room, or possibly as a dining room, you may need to compromise with a softer floorcovering, or to soften the harder type with rush matting or rugs (easily washable). Many floorcoverings do tend to be slippery when wet, so it is vitally important to know which are before installing them, particularly if there are young or elderly people in the house, and the space is to be used as a family or living room. In the right setting, some artificial turf-by-the-yard can be a most effective floor treatment.

As with any part of the home, before the floor can be laid, the subfloor must be in good condition. Smooth, level and free from dampness – and in certain cases a new subfloor or screed or damproof vapour barrier may have to be laid (see page 76). It is wise to seek expert advice on this before construction or alterations begin.

In this striking glass extension, bright blue paintwork is an original choice of colour emphasizing the shape of the windows and the unusual cut-away shape that serves as a doorway to the rest of the house.

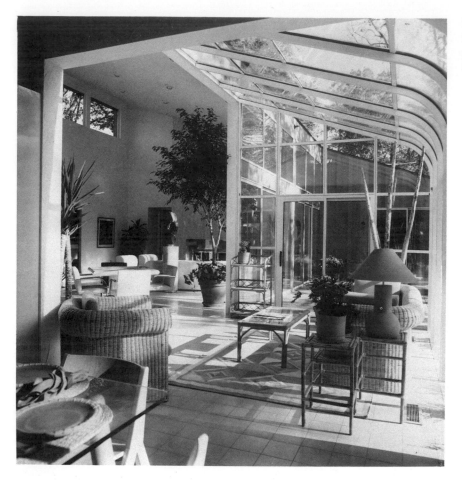

To emphasize the additional space created by adding on a conservatory, continue the original flooring of the adjacent room through into the new extension.

Ceramic and quarry tiles are one of the most practical floorings and these now come in a wide range of shapes, sizes, patterns and colours, which can echo the basic style and design. When choosing tiles, make sure they are flooring quality and not intended only for walls (some manufacturers make ranges suitable for both), and remember the highly glazed ones are very slippery when wet.

If the room has a lot of glass and will be subject to extremes of temperature, consider a frost-proof tile. Some manufacturers make a special range, while others will frost-proof their tiles if you stipulate this at the time of ordering. If the room leads onto a patio or terrace, you could carry the same tiles throughout the two areas. One point to remember is that some quarry tiles are very porous and when used indoors should be sealed to prevent stains from sinking in. The supplier or manufacturer will advise you on the porosity of the tiles and the best sealant to use.

Paving slabs are thicker, heavier and usually larger than tiles, and

One of the advantages of tiled floors is the variety of patterns that can be achieved to suit an individual's taste and budget. Here a mixture of triangular and square quarry tiles in three colour-ways make up a dramatic pattern which harmonizes with the rest of the decor.

come in natural and reconstituted stone. There are several different sizes and shapes available and quite a few are coloured in soft pinks, greens, gold, beige, brown, etc. Choose a colour or several colours to blend with your decor and to show off the plants to advantage. Unusual patterns can be created with them: chequerboard, borders, diagonal designs, herringbone pattern, stripes, and many more. Again, this type of paving can be carried on to the patio, and is naturally frost-proof.

Mosaics – these small irregularly-shaped tiles come in a wide range of colours and glazes; some as simple terracotta, others as marble mosaics. The type which comes on a mesh backing is easier to handle, but does not leave much scope for original design. There are specialist companies that will design and then pre-form mosaics into panels, which they then install in situ. This is well worth considering in a very special conservatory, particularly one which combines a pool.

Similarly, many of the ceramic suppliers and manufacturers will design a floor individually and will supply it ready numbered for your builder to lay, or they will come and lay it. It might be possible to include a companion mural for the wall in either mosaic or ceramic.

Marble is very expensive, but as a classic flooring is the most elegant. It comes in various natural colours, with a highly polished surface, usually as marble slabs, but some marbles are polished after laying. There are some less expensive marbles – both a reconstituted type and one where marble chippings are impregnated in a base material. Terrazzo is similar, and is less expensive, and it can be obtained in various textures, colours and effects. However, both of these are very slippery when wet. Either type can be taken out onto the patio or terrace to create a vista effect.

Paving bricks – old ones, new ones and specially faced ones can give a rich, warm look to the floor, and are usually non-slip. They can be laid in many interesting ways to form patterns such as herringbone, and if two or three differently coloured bricks are selected, it is possible to create some very unusual effects. Again, the same flooring could be taken outside onto a patio or path.

Cork tiles look attractive in this setting and these are available in the characteristic natural golden and brown colouring, and also as coloured cork. The latter consists of very thin slivers of cork laid over a base colour (red, green, blue, and milky white) and this 'grins' through the cork layer. These different colours can be used to create a highly original floor, and can be laid in several of the ways previously suggested to create a design.

These pots of plants are wisely placed in drip trays to prevent splashes and drips marking the parquet flooring.

Cork tiles must always be properly sealed, particularly when they are being used in a situation where the floor could get damp, because when cork gets wet, it swells and the tiles push up, creating an uneven surface. The pre-sealed type of cork tile is best for use in such an area. Cork cannot be used outside.

Wood of all types – floorboards, woodblock, wood mosaic, parquet, hardwood strip, etc. can show off plants and foliage to advantage, but wood is not an ideal flooring for use in a space subject to damp and humidity. If you do decide to use it, then make sure it is properly sealed with a transparent polyurethane sealer which can be matt, semi-matt or gloss finished.

Rubber is flexible and fairly soft underfoot, and comes in several different forms: as tiles and sheet; with non-slip textures; and in several primary colours and black and marbled effects. Rubber does tend to perish if it gets wet continually and can be affected by strong sunlight, so seek advice before using it. In many cases it may be necessary to have a special vapour-proof membrane on top of the subfloor and under the rubber.

Linoleum is making a come-back as a flooring, and is mostly available as tiles of various thickness (gauge) and several sizes. There are still a few sheet linoleums available. The colour range is good, and usually the texture is marbled. Again, it is possible to make patterns and designs with different coloured tiles, and you can also inlay patterns into linoleum. It can be slippery when wet, and also some types can fade in strong sunlight, so again seek advice for your particular floor area.

Vinyl comes in several guises – as the cushioned, and very bouncy underfoot type, which is usually in sheet form and in several different widths; as a non-cushioned sheet; as tiles, which include cushioned and non-cushioned and peel-and-stick-down type. There is a wide range of colours, patterns and styles, including many which simulate brick, paving slabs and ceramics. Vinyl is fairly waterproof, so long as it is stuck down to the subfloor and all the joins are properly sealed, and is not too slippery when wet. It is a good choice for an inexpensive flooring.

Carpet is not a practical flooring but carpet tiles are a possibility. They tend to be of a felted construction, which does not absorb spills so readily, but they can be taken up individually (and replaced if necessary) for drying or cleaning. They come in a range of colours, and some patterns, and in various sizes – usually 9- or 18-in (23- or 46-cm) squares. There is a special type of carpet tile intended for use in kitchens, which is even more hard-wearing and stands up to staining and even grease spills, but the colours and designs are somewhat limited.

Traditional quarry tiles are an attractive feature of this delightful garden room. Although expensive to install, they are very resilient and will still look unspoiled after many years of wear.

Natural textures create a
pleasing mellow atmosphere, particularly
when combined with plants. In this
conservatory, the walls have been stripped
of plaster to expose the brickwork.

Matting of various types – rush, sisal, coconut, coir, even woven plastic – can be used, particularly to soften a harder flooring. Some washable rugs might also be considered. These mattings and rugs, produced in a square or oblong form (some mattings would need to be seamed) can make an attractive softer covering for a 'conversation group' where chairs or settees are placed together in a seating arrangement, round a coffee table.

Walls

Wall treatments in this part of the home can be much more unusual and exciting, and need not be as perfectly finished as in other rooms. An original rough brick or stone wall can give a mellow look and a warm texture to the room, and a similar effect can be created with facing bricks or stone. Wooden or plastic garden trellis can be pinned to this (and to many other types of wall finish) and used to train climbing plants.

If you want to create an elegant atmosphere a patterned wallcovering can be used. Paper is not the most practical material to use in a humid room, so use a vinyl wallcovering. Make sure the seams are butt-joined and stuck down firmly. As so much of the wall area is likely to be glass, if you want a definitely patterned look, consider one of the co-ordinated ranges which have companion fabrics, blinds and wallcoverings. Select the pattern and colour to blend with the style which you want the room to have, or to emphasize the architectural style. Avoid silky or fussy textures which look more at home in a drawing room than a conservatory.

Walls can, of course, be painted with a gloss, matt or semi-matt finish but garden rooms are, as discussed on p. 47, ideal places for painted wall patterns or murals. This kind of treatment can be used to make the area twice as large.

Similar effects can be made with a panel of patterned ceramic tiles. You can also do-your-own mosaic with broken bottle glass and ceramic (or other) chippings, to create a picture or a pattern.

Wood cladding mounted ranch-style (horizontally), or vertically, or in panels, can be a very effective wall treatment for this type of room. The simple tongue-and-groove type can be painted, or stained and sealed, or left natural and sealed. Other, more decorative woods may be used, and finished according to taste and the type of wood.

Cork is another suitable wall covering. The thick sheet or tile wall-cork is a splendid insulation, and because it is soft, plants can be pinned to it and trained to grow in unusual shapes.

Furniture and furnishings

Once the basic style for the garden room has been decided, try to select furniture to suit. If you have an older type of building with tall graceful arched or gothic-shaped windows, and lots of white 'structure', try to echo the elegance of gracious living from a previous era. White cast-iron or cast-aluminium furniture, which reflects the period flavour, will be very much in keeping for chairs and tables. Avoid the tubular steel and plastic reproductions, and if working to a tight budget, look for bargains in junk shops, at jumble or garage sales, or in builders' yards. White gloss spray-paint and a new marble or glass top to a table will all help to give the room an authentic nineteenth- or twentieth-century look.

Accessories should also be in keeping – attractive, delicate filigree cast-iron stoves; shiny ceramic cachepots; dramatically decorated aspidistra pots and stands; white or terracotta tubs for trees and plants will all set the right note.

Cane and bamboo upholstered chairs and settees, with matching glass- or caned-topped tables are also in keeping with this style of room. They can be natural coloured, stained a dark brown or in a colour, and sometimes cane and bamboo is painted white. Keep to the natural colours (browns and greens) or white, rather than the bright reds, orange and blue, for an authentic look.

Choose fabric for the cushions with the correct period flavour – flowing floral design of the William Morris Art Nouveau type; a pretty glazed chintz with fruit, flowers and birds; a traditional trellis design, or a trailing ivyleaf one – and again stick to the more natural and neutral colours, or the authentic ones of the period. Avoid harsh primary colours and modern floral prints or those with geometric patterns.

Upholstery fabrics, apart from suiting the style of the furniture, which in turn suits the style of the room, should be as practical as possible, which means fully washable or at least dry cleanable, unaffected by strong sunlight, and rot-proof. Make sure that all chair or cushion covers are easily removable by using zips, ties or velcro.

If the garden room is more like a 1920s or 1930s loggia or verandah, it can be given the colonial 'Graham Greene' look, with bamboo and rattan screens and furniture. Try to find cane furniture of the period and cheer it up if necessary with a coat of paint or a spray of clear gloss polyurethane varnish.

Glass and white wrought-iron tables create a period feel, as do big squashy chintz-covered sofas; while woven cane-sided chairs and settees or folding club or film director-style deck chairs will all

*Modern 'hi-tech' areas of glass require
careful accessorizing if they are to maintain
their stark appearance. Here, primary-
coloured designer furniture together with
slatted room dividers and tubular steel
stair rail are ideal.*

131

help to create the desired image. But again, use fabrics such as chintzes, stylized flower heads, trellis patterns and Art Deco designs or plain linen and canvas.

A very modern extension can be given the hi-tech treatment by using brightly painted tubular steel or plastic-coated scaffold tubes to make staging for plants, and matching angular furniture. This is the type of room in which to use sharply contrasted colours, possibly on the floor, in tiles laid chequerboard fashion or diagonally, and bold geometric designs.

Do not underestimate the use of screens. These can be used to divide the area visually, as well as making discreet corners, and plants can be trained up and down them. There are portable screens of the rattan type, or wrought iron can be 'twisted' into a suitable grid. Basic screens can be made from battens with garden trellis pinned to them, or from bamboo canes, fixed criss-cross fashion. Tubular steel can be used in the same way for the more modern type of room setting.

Window dressing

Most garden and sun rooms or extensions have large windows, and vast areas of glass. This may be double or even triple glazed to avoid heat loss, although, in many cases, single glazing is the norm. If you are installing two thicknesses of glass, think about the window treatment before ordering it, as it makes sense, in some cases, to have blinds incorporated between the two layers.

Large areas of glass always need some form of screen, either inside or out to keep out strong sun during very hot weather, as well as conserving heat inside the room at night, and giving some privacy after the lamps are lit.

Blinds come in various colours, patterns, types and sizes. The Venetian sort can have vertical or horizontal slats, mostly made of thin metal, but wooden Venetian blinds are still made, and can be just right in this type of room. There is a special type made for angled and sloping windows, which can be particularly practical in a garden room where part of the roof is made from sloping glass. The vertical type are frequently made from textured fabric, and can have angled, or short and long slats to fit sloping windows, or to make a 'hole' to accommodate projections. Many of these can be fitted between two layers of glass with control from the inside, and the angled type can have remote control.

There are special pleated insulated blinds, which have an attractive gauzy finish and prevent heat loss as well as the sun's rays from fading the fabric or damaging plants inside the room.

Not all furnishings and fittings need be expensive – cheerful fans provide cheap temporary shading for plants on a window-sill, and can be moved easily to suit the changing seasons.

Rattan and pinoleum blinds, wood-strip, and old-fashioned greenhouse blinds (made from thin green canes) are also suitable for window screening.

Fabric blinds can also be used to soften stark areas of glass, and these come in various forms and fabrics, and as Roman, Austrian and festoon blinds. The fabric can co-ordinate with the rest of the decorations or contrast with them, and many of these blinds come in very soft sheers and voiles, which can be draped.

Awnings can be fitted outside the windows, and consequently do double duty, screening the patio as well as the glass. These come in various types and sizes and are made in several different kinds of strong fabric. There are also exterior shutters and roller screens in metal, wood and heavy-duty plastic suitable for use as exterior screens.

Curtains may be used but in many cases, depending on the window type and the actual use the room is put to, they look rather out of place. Floor-to-ceiling and wall-to-wall curtains work well on some sliding patio doors, and it is wise to line and interline them when possible, to give extra insulation.

Net drapes can soften a stark window, and some of the beautifully patterned net panels look very effective in a 'traditional' conservatory which is used partly for living or dining. They can be combined with Venetian blinds to give greater privacy at night. Semi-transparent sheers and voiles can be equally effective, and look good trimmed with a patterned border of fabric which matches the decor or upholstery fabrics.

Stained glass looks very effective, particularly with sunlight shining through it, casting a colourful pattern on the floor or wall. Some of the older buildings may already have stained glass windows or panels, or you can buy panels to place inside plain glazed windows. Try not to screen these from view.

Lighting

Lighting your extension or garden room will, to some extent, depend on its function. If it is to be used as a dining area and a sitting room, then the lighting will have to be chosen just as it would for the same rooms in the home, with good lighting for the dining table (possibly a rise-and-fall fitting over the centre of the table) and the serving area, and the rest of the room subdued, with background illumination. If you wish to read, sew or chat, then pools of light can be provided by strategically placed lamps, which could be adjustable.

The light fittings should blend with the architectural style of the

room and echo its furnishings. In the traditional type of conservatory, furnished with cane, if you decide on a ceiling fan (see p. 140) this can be combined with lights of various types. In a room of Victorian or Edwardian style you might use real or converted oil lamps or converted gas brackets; and for an unusual table light, billiard- or pool-room lighting could be adapted – the glass-shaded variety could be particularly effective.

Try to light plants for maximum effect and to bring out the full effect of luxuriant foliage. Coloured lighting gives an extra dramatic touch, but check with the supplier to see whether this will affect plant growth. Where possible carry the lighting through into the garden or onto the patio, but ensure that cables for the outside, or if combined with a pool, are the proper exterior heavy-duty sort, and are absolutely safe. Always have this type of lighting installed by a professional electrican.

Atmosphere

Use your lighting to create atmosphere: to focus attention on accessories; to make the most of the room's salient features; to emphasize interesting textures on a stone or brick wall; and to dramatize niches, statuary, pools or groups or plants. If you have incorporated a fish tank, make sure that this too is cleverly illuminated, so it glows like a jewel.

Important accessories should be lit for maximum impact. They can be spotlit, floodlit, or lit by downlighters or uplighters (possibly placed under a glass-topped table on which plants are massed). In a glass-roofed conservatory, it should be possible to fix track to the ribs of the roof, and have spotlights slotted into the track at regular intervals, angled towards the items to be illuminated. Sometimes, back lighting provides the right degree of drama. Choose a feathery plant, a beautifully-shaped shrub, or an interesting piece of statuary as possible subjects. Wall lights of a suitable shape and size can provide good background lighting, and will emphasize the wall's texture – or, light the wall from its base. Another idea might be to use a false pelmet, cornice or coving across the top of a wall to conceal strip lighting.

Lighting can be used to bathe the whole area in diffused light, or to 'wash' a wall with colour, and for a really theatrical touch, projections could be used to create an impression of sky and clouds, sun on sand or snow, and stars twinkling in a velvety sky.

If the garden room has large patio doors, screened by blinds, consider using diffused strip lighting, hidden behind a pelmet, placed to conceal the track at the top of the blind. If you have

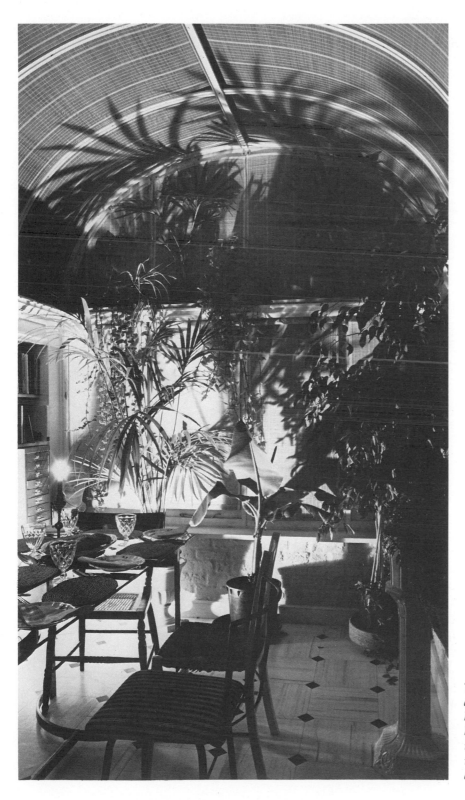

This inviting dining-area owes its dramatic atmosphere to the use of spotlights highlighting certain areas. Note also how linoleum has been cleverly cut and interspersed with smaller black squares to reproduce the look of traditional flooring at a much lower cost.

137

decided to have a collection of glass, on shelves across a window, try to illuminate this from above, again with concealed pelmet lighting at the top of the window.

For a special party or dinner, try the simplest lighting of all. Use oil lamps, candles inside storm lanterns or glass jars, or even stuck into bottles, or string fairy lights between trees, shrubs and plants. There are special bulbs which simulate flickering candle flames which can be used in lanterns and lamps if preferred.

Finally, when planning the lighting remember that it is just as important when seen from the outside, particularly if the extension is almost fully glazed – fittings which appear concealed from inside should not look ugly from the outside.

Accessories

The accessories and finishing touches to the garden room are just as important as they are in other areas of the home. Again they need to echo the general mood and style of the room to give it personality.

Old chimney pots (seek them out in builders' yards) are highly decorative and make ideal plant containers. So do earthenware jars (originally used for pickles, wine making, or salting beans), old hip baths and copper containers. There is an enormous selection of plant containers on the market nowadays in a wide range of materials including terracotta, stone (reconstituted or the real thing) metal, wooden and plastic all intended for outdoor and indoor use. Attach wheels or casters to the base of large containers so that they can be moved easily for routine maintenance, or brought forward into prominence at particular times of the year.

Look for unusual containers for plants, trees and shrubs such as decorative rattan or metal bird cages which look very attractive when hung from the ceiling, filled with trailing plants. They can, of course, also contain birds, and these may well be an integral part of your scheme. Fish too, swimming in tanks or a pool, will also give added interest to this type of room.

Simple, natural items can also look attractive in a garden room – an old tree trunk or piece of driftwood can have plants trained round it. Pebbles and stones or coloured gravel piled round the base of plants or containers, or set into part of the floor, will set off foliage to advantage.

Statues and pottery can also look dramatic, especially if they are properly lit. Lighting is all important in helping to create an atmosphere, and interesting accessories should be highlighted.

On the first storey of this modern home, plants thrive in the natural light from the glass-roof, and by night are illuminated by spotlights. The ground floor kitchen benefits from concealed strip lights, more suited to a working area.

Many local potteries will make special containers and decorative items to order.

If you have one of the older, elegant types of conservatory you might consider using one of the large, slowly revolving ceiling fans which are efficient, inexpensive to operate and also add a touch of the exotic. Electrically operated, they are now made in painted metal or lacquered brass, and can be combined with lighting fittings.

Staging and support for plants can be provided in several unusual and different ways, apart from the conventional greenhouse staging. Try adapting slatted trestle tables, which are as practical as they are easy to move, or tubular scaffolding and simple flexible shelving systems intended for kitchen storage. Several of the wire racks or containers intended for kitchen cupboards can also be adapted for displaying plants, while hanging baskets, suspended from the ceiling, one under the other, or stepped, look decorative and make three-dimensional use of the space.

Old-fashioned plant holders such as these (below) are currently enjoying a revival in popularity and can still be found in markets and junk stalls. Alternatively, new reproduction pieces are readily available.

Pools and water gardens

Provided there is sufficient space, a pool, complete with fountain and constantly running water, or even a cascade effect over rocks, can provide a cool and relaxing atmosphere. It could contain fish and water-loving plants could be grown round it for added interest. However, if space is at a premium, consider a very small static pool or a very simple fountain.

Remember that in a home where there are children water can be dangerous so make sure the young are supervised or that the pool is adequately protected.

To help you decide what kind of pool or fountain to have, visit some water-garden centres, or some good garden centres, to see exactly what is available. Pools can be made in several ways, and the most basic is a complete preformed system. This can be a liner intended for sinking into the earth, which may not be practical in the garden room, although you can put it on the floor and build up earth and rocks round it. Some preformed systems are available for use on top of the earth or, of course, you could use concrete or a stone trough.

Alternatively, if you are very short of space, a small tub pool might be the answer. You can make one from half a beer barrel, or use one of thetubs sold in garden centres for plants. Coat the inside with bituminous paint, fill with water, a few fish and some aquatic plants, which might include a pygmy water lily or umbrella sedge.

An old church stand (right) makes an unusual plant holder and an interesting feature. Many old pieces of furniture can be used in this way with plants strategically placed to camouflage any defects.

Flexible liners, made from butyl (a type of rubber), PVC or polythene (polyethylene), are frequently used in garden pools. These are usually to line a hole in the ground, so are only practical in a conservatory if you are able to sink them below floor level, or to build up earth round them. Because the life expectancy of polythene and PVC is only between two to ten years – depending on its thickness and the care you have taken during its installation – so you must expect leakages after a few years.

Glass-fibre or rigid plastic pools are more sensible, but again are usually intended for sinking into the ground, so select an attractive shape which can have rocks, plant containers, etc. built up round it. Alternatively, use a preformed concrete, stone or rigid plastic 'patio' pool, of the type made to be freestanding.

Fountains and cascades add extra life to a pool by providing constant movement. They need to be operated by a suitable electric pump. The type and size necessary will depend on the size of the pool, so ask about this when buying the pool. Make sure that it is powerful enough to keep the water circulating, and to raise the water high enough for the fountain to be effective. The most usual type is a submersible pump which recirculates existing water. These are small, encased in plastic and fitted with waterproof cable – most garden centres and aquatic equipment shops will stock several different kinds and sizes, and for indoor use it is particularly important to buy a quiet one.

Fountains, complete with their own recirculating system, are available in stone or reconstituted stone, and often incorporate a small statue. These look particularly effective in a conservatory where space is limited.

Because water and electricity are a dangerous combination, do seek the help of a competent electrician to install a pump or fountain, and at the same time, ask about illuminating the plants and the water feature in the garden room; remember well-lit pools and fountains always look romantic.

The ultimate skyline conservatory fitting –
a hot-tub

Plants for the Conservatory

There are many hundreds of plants suitable for growing in an indoor environment, and the lists that follow describe a selection of the best. The plants are divided into five categories. The first three describe plants for various temperature and humidity regimes, the fourth lists plants for indoor pools, while the last suggests plants for use outside the garden room.

Most indoor plants are remarkably tolerant whether from jungle or desert. Many will survive lower temperatures for short periods, while others can cope with higher temperatures. Few, however – other than water plants – will survive over-watering, and most dislike draughts. Humidity is required by a large number of plants (this can often be provided locally), while cacti and succulents thrive in surprisingly dry conditions.

Great care must be taken in providing adequate heating, draught proofing, air circulation, humidity control and lighting. Under glass, full sun may severely scorch the plants, so ensure there is adequate shading. This is not as daunting as it sounds for, following the cultural instructions given under each plant, you should be as successful as the owners of the conservatories illustrated elsewhere in this book. More information can be found in books dealing with indoor plants, and many nurseries, garden centres and stores provide growing instructions with their plants.

The medium in which you grow the plants is an important factor in their health, and two basic types are mentioned in the lists. The loam-based one is made by mixing 7 parts (by volume) of sterilized loam with 3 parts of peat and 2 parts of coarse sand. To each bushel (about 36 litres) of this mix, add 8oz (227gr) of fertilizer, and 1½oz (43gr) of powdered chalk. The peat-based (or loamless) mix consists of 1 part of peat and 1 part of coarse sand (again by volume), and to each bushel of this add the following: 3oz (85gr) ammonium nitrate, 1oz (28gr) potassium sulphate, 3oz (85gr) hoof and horn, 2oz (57gr) magnesium limestone, 4oz (113gr) chalk, and 2oz (57gr)

Reminiscent of Victorian times, this plant-filled conservatory in Melbourne, Australia shows how well plants can be grown when their temperature and humidity needs are properly met.

calcium phosphate. Soil could be used from the garden for the loam-based mix but unless you have facilities for sterilizing it, any saving of money will be more than offset by the problems caused with the introduction of soil-borne pests and diseases. For a small number of plants it is better and easier to purchase the ready-made commercial mixes used for lime-hating plants, and some plants, as mentioned in the lists, require more sand than is in the purchased mixes.

Gardening indoors is a very pleasurable occupation that can be done whatever the weather outside, and the flowers or foliage of any of the listed plants will give an extra dimension to even the simplest home extension.

To help you select plants for your particular conservatory or garden room the plants have been grouped together in lists, each of which is suitable for a particular temperature and humidity regime.

List 1 (p. 146-56) Plants for heated conservatories and extensions used mainly as plant rooms. In these structures plants are more important than people. Conditions must be humid and the temperature should rarely be allowed to fall below 60°F(16°C).

List 2 (p. 156-73) Plants for slightly heated extensions and living rooms. Here, plants and people have equal importance. The level of humidity is less than that of List 1, and the temperature is usually kept above 50°F(10°C).

List 3 (p. 173-80) Plants for unheated conservatories, extensions and living rooms. These are suitable for places in which the temperature may occasionally fall to freezing point, but where some form of heat is used during prolonged cold spells.

List 4 (p. 180-81) Indoor water plants. The plants listed here are suitable for decorative purposes in indoor pools of differing temperature regimes.

List 5 (p. 180-85) Outdoor plants. These are hardy subjects for planting outside conservaties and garden rooms to provide screens and decorative effect when viewed from within or from the outside.

The **bold** figures which appear beside some plant headings refer to the numbered illustrations.

List 1 Plants for heated conservatories and extensions used mainly as plant rooms
In these structures plants are more important than people. Conditions must be humid and the temperature should rarely be allowed to fall below 60°F(16°C).

ACHIMENES (monkey-faced or orchid pansy, hot water plant)
The many common names, of which the three above are only a sample, indicate the popularity of these plants which bear their flowers in abundance. Keep them warm, not less than 60°F(16°C), and moist, with highly humid surroundings while they are growing and flowering. After flowering dry their tubers off and store them in a warm place, not less than about 54°F(12°C), overwinter. Repot in spring, when the tubers may be divided to increase your plants, and start them into growth again. For preference use one of the all-peat mixes. The following are a small selection of the many species, and varieties, which originate from tropical America. *A. erecta (A. coccinea* cupid's bower) has scarlet red flowers from late summer to mid-winter. A compact plant to 1½ft(45cm) tall. *A. heterophylla*, has orange-red to scarlet flowers with a yellow throat. It grows to about 1ft(30cm) tall usually but the variety 'Little Beauty' is smaller and has deep pink flowers. Both flower from mid-summer. *A. longiflora*, has lilac to purple flowers, often with a white eye. The stems are trailing to 1ft(30cm) making it a lovely plant for a hanging basket. There are several varieties, two of the most striking being 'Alba', with white, yellow eyed flowers with a purple line contrasting well on each lobe, and 'Major', which has flowers as much as 3in(7.5cm) across, yellow throated with light violet lobes.

ADIANTUM (maidenhair fern)   1
There are many species of maidenhair fern and some of them make elegant and graceful pot plants. They should be shaded from direct sun but do like warmth, 60°F(16°C) minimum. Keep them moist but not too wet. Grow them in a peat-based mix and increase them by division when needed. *A. raddianum (A. cuneatum* delta maidenhair) is a small plant, the fronds 6-12in(15-30cm) long. It has a number of excellent varieties, including 'Fritz-Luth' ('Fritz-Luthii') with the leaflets set at varying angles, and

'Fragrantissimum' with scented foliage. *A. tenerum* (brittle maidenhair) has a splendid variety 'Farleyense', the dainty fronds having ruffled, overlapping fan shaped leaflets. It needs plenty of room as the fronds may grow 3ft(90cm) long and up to 2ft(60cm) wide.

AECHMEA (air pine or living vase)
Aechmeas are rosette-forming plants rather like pineapples in leaf. Striking-coloured flower stems grow out of the centre and often have contrasting coloured flowers. The plants usually die after flowering but by then will usually have sent up new shoots from the base. Detach these and grow them on. Grow in small pots of peat-based mixes kept moist but not too wet and keep the centre of the leaf rosette filled with water – preferably soft. Most will tolerate lower temperatures but over 60°F(16°C) is best. *A. chantinii*, up to 3ft(1m) high, has green leaves banded with silver and orange-red flower stems with yellow flowers. *A. fasciata (Billbergia rhodocyanea* urn plant) has grey-green leaves banded with silver, pink flower stems with bluish flowers that turn red, and is about 2ft(60cm) tall.

AESCHYNANTHUS (*Trichosporum* basket plant)
Perhaps the most useful are the trailing species which give an exotic look to hanging baskets where their brilliant red flowers are shown to advantage. They will tolerate temperatures lower than 60°F(16°C) but need warmth and humidity though they should be shaded from direct sun. Grow them in an all-peat mix which should be kept only just moist in winter but watered freely in the summer. All the following are trailing, the leaves cascading down on stems about 2ft(60cm) long. *A. marmoratus (A. zebrinus* zebra basket vine) has exceptional flowers of green marked with brown and is often grown for its foliage, the leaves being dark green netted with yellow. *A. radicans (A. lobbianus* lipstick vine) has brilliant red flowers blotched with yellow at the base. *A. speciosus*

has bright orange red flowers shading to a yellow throat.

AGLAONEMA (chinese evergreens)

The tough leaves of these evergreens are usually variegated with silver markings which differ according to the species. Slow growing they will thrive in fairly poor light and in temperatures which may fall as low as 55°F(13°C). All-peat mixes are best for these good houseplants. Shade from sun, and keep a humid atmosphere. *A. commutatum* is 9-12in(23-30cm) high and has lance-shaped leaves, dark green with silver. *A. costatum*, spotted evergreen, has very dark leaves with a white midrib and white spots, and is 6in(15cm) tall. *A. crispum* (painted drop tongue) has large leaves heavily splashed with greyish silver and grows up to 4ft(1.2m) tall.

ALLAMANDA

The golden trumpet or common allamanda, *A. cathartica*, is an evergreen clambering plant which may reach 15ft(4.6m) or more in the wild. It, and its varieties, have large yellow flowers in summer and autumn. Grow them in a border or very large pots of a loam-based commercial mix and feed them during the growing season. Keep them much drier over winter and start them into growth the following spring. This is also the time to repot if required, and when cuttings may be taken. Keep shaded from direct sun but in a temperature above 55°F(13°C) at all times. The variety 'Grandiflora' has pale yellow flowers while 'Hendersonii' has rich gold flowers.

ANGRAECUM

These leafy tropical orchids have gracefully arching stems of fragrant flowers. Keep them in humid, warm conditions. Grow them in orchid pots or baskets filled with equal parts of sphagnum moss and osmunda fibre. Keep them moist and fed with a weak solution of plant food during the growing season but drier in winter. Side shoots may be detached in spring and grown on. *A. infundibulare*, a small climbing or trailing plant, 2-5ft(60-150cm), with large solitary flowers, 3½in(9cm) across, pale yellow, white and green based. *A. superbum* (*A. eburneum*) is strong growing to 4ft(1.2m) or more, with many green and white, 4in(10cm) flowers on long stems.

ANTHURIUM (tailflower)

Two species of the hundreds of these exotic tropical plants provide the most popular indoor plants. They require warmth and humidity but not direct sun and should be grown in a half-and-half mixture of sphagnum moss and a peat-based potting mix. Keep moist but not wet and drier in winter. Divide when necessary or required in winter. *A. andreanum* (flamingo lily or oilcloth flower) reaches 1½ft(46cm) and has flowers of deep orange to scarlet with a yellow spadix and hybrids with rose, pink and white flowers. *A. scherzeranum* (flamingo flower or pigtail plant) has brilliant shiny scarlet flowers with a yellow, twisted spadix and is only half as tall.

ARISTOLOCHIA

The calico flower, *A. elegans*, is a striking climbing plant with large and curious flowers, which may reach 20ft(6m). The flowers, 4½in(12cm) across, are white netted purple outside and chocolate-purple netted white inside. Keep warm but shaded from sun. Grow in any good commercial mix which should be kept moist.

BROWALLIA

One of the best browallias in cultivation is the sapphire flower, *B. speciosa* 'Major', which has deep blue flowers and grows up to 4ft(1.2m) tall. It may be raised annually from seed sown in spring for summer flowering or autumn for flowers in winter. As soon as the seedlings are large enough prick them out into individual 3in(7.5cm) pots of potting mix and pot them on as required until they are in 6in(15cm) pots. When flower buds appear feed with liquid fertilizer every fortnight. A white-flowered variety 'Silver Bells' is sometimes available.

CALADIUM (elephant's ear)

Caladiums have splendidly patterned and coloured leaves often on long arching stems. Grow them in peat-based mixes, well watered and fed fortnightly when the leaves are expanded but drier at other times and store the tubers dry over winter. Keep warm at all times, even store at 55°F(13°C). A number of hybrids are available under the group name *C.* × *hortulanum* though they may be listed as varieties of *C. bicolor*. They include 'Candidum', large white leaves veined green, 'Frieda Hemple', red leaves with darker veins and green margined, and 'Seagull' has dark green leaves with white veins. All are about 9-15in(23-35cm) tall.

CALATHEA 2
Beautiful foliage plants for a warm and humid atmosphere, calatheas form clumps or tufts of leaves. Shade them from direct sun and grow them in a peat-based mix to which has been added ⅓ part of grit or coarse sharp sand. Repot and increase by division in spring. *C. makoyana* (peacock plant) has creamy-green leaves with fine green veins and green oval blotches between on the upper surface with a similar pattern in crimson below. *C. zebrina* (zebra plant) has velvet green leaves veined in yellowish green and purple below. Both grow between 1½-2ft(45-61cm) tall.

CATTLEYA
Splendid tropical, epiphytic orchids, many of which have large flowers and huge pseudobulbs. They require a humid and warm atmosphere. Grow in orchid pots or baskets filled with a mix of ⅔ osmunda fibre and ⅓ sphagnum moss. Keep shaded from sun through spring and summer but keep cooler and in full light then. Divide in spring or summer if required. Many species and hybrids are grown including the following. *C. citrina* (tulip cattleya) is a pendent species so best in a basket, with fragrant yellow flowers and is tolerant of cooler conditions, leaves up to 10in/25cm long. *C. dowiana (C. labiata dowiana* queen cattleya) only has one large leaf and flowers of yellow with a purple lip and needs warmth, about 1ft(30cm) tall. *C. labiata* (autumn cattleya) has pale rosy lilac flowers with a crimson violet lip and yellow throat, about 16in(40cm) tall. *C. trianaei* (Christmas orchid) is variable with flowers from rose to white, purple lipped and with a yellow throat, may grow 1½ft(45cm) tall.

CHAMAEDOREA
The most popular species of palm, *C. elegans (Collinia elegans, Neanthe bella* parlour or good luck palm), has graceful fronds of arching leaves which may, in time reach 8ft(2.4m) on a 4-6ft(1.2-1.8m) plant. Keep warm but shaded from strong sun and in a humid atmos-phere. Grow in loam- or peat-based mixes kept moist but not overwatered. Propagate by spring-sown seed.

CISSUS
A number of excellent climbing or trailing *Cissus* species make splendid indoor plants including the beautiful *C. discolor*, which, despite its names of rex begonia vine, trailing or climbing begonia is not related to *Begonia*. The lovely velvet-green leaves have silver to pale pink markings above but are purple beneath. It may grow to 10ft(3m) but needs a very warm and humid atmosphere. Grow in moist loam- or peat-based mixes. Increase by tip cuttings in summer or seed.

CLERODENDRUM (glory bower)
Magnificent flowering shrubs and climbers for warm, humid atmospheres, clerodendrums should be shaded from strong sun. Grow them in loam- or peat-based mixes in large pots or an indoor border. Increase by summer cuttings or spring sown seed. *C. paniculatum* (pagoda flower) is a shrub with clusters of scarlet flowers and grows 3-4ft(90-120cm). *C. thomso-niae* (bleeding heart vine) a fine climber with flowers of white and crimson may reach 10-12ft(3-3.7m).

COLUMNEA 3
Really lovely plants for hanging baskets, the orange to scarlet crimson flowers look like sheets of flame on well grown plants. Warmth, humidity in summer, but shade from direct sun, are essential. Grow in moist but not over wet mix made of ⅓ grit or very coarse sharp sand added to a peat-based commercial mix. Liquid feed every two weeks during the sum-mer. Increase by seed in spring or cuttings of unflowered shoots then or in summer. *C. × banksii*, scarlet flowers on 2-2½ft(60-75cm) stems. *C. gloriosa*, yellow throated scarlet flowers on stems 3ft(90cm) or more long and set with velvety purplish leaves which are even more deeply coloured in the variety 'Super-ba' ('Purpurea'). *C.* 'Stavanger', with 2ft(60cm) or more long stems has flowers of brilliant deep red lightening to orange at their bases.

CORDYLINE
An exotic plant with bronzy-green leaves, *C. termina-lis (Dracaena terminalis* tree of heaven, ti tree), grows

up to about 10ft(3m) in time. It needs a warm and humid environment to thrive and should be grown in large pots of well draining loam-based mix, add grit or sharp sand if necessary. Increase by seed in spring, cuttings in summer. Several good varieties are available with different coloured leaves, including 'Tricolor' with leaves of red, pink, cream and green.

CROSSANDRA (firecracker flower)
Fine shrubby plants with clusters of brightly coloured flowers, crossandras make good pot plants if they can be kept warm and slightly humid, though protected from direct sun. Grow preferably in peat-based mixes and feed regularly during the summer and early autumn when well established. Repot in spring and cut the plants back to keep them bushy by about a half or more if very straggly. Increase in spring to summer by cuttings, or by seed in spring. *C. infundibuliformis (C. undulifolia)* is a beautiful plant with flowers of salmon to bright orange, which may grow to 3ft(90cm); *C. nilotica* is rather similar but with more downy leaves and shorter growing to about 2ft(60cm) *C. pungens* is similar to *C. nilotica* but has denser heads of flowers.

CRYPTANTHUS (earth star)
Mainly grown for their superbly patterned and coloured rosettes of leaves, earth stars usually have white flowers which are rather insignificant. They need warmth and humidity and to be grown in shallow containers, such as half pots or pans. Use a conventional mix with additional sphagnum moss or a peat-based mix. Increase by offsets. *C. acaulis* (starfish plant, green earth star) small green-leaved rosette up to 6in(15cm) across, white flowers. *C. bivittatus* has rosettes up to 15in(38cm) across, the leaves brownish-green with two coppery-pink stripes along each. *C. bromeloides* grows more upright, the rosettes up to 14in(35cm) across, and has a strikingly coloured foliage variety *tricolor* (rainbow star) with leaves striped in green and cream and with pink margins. *C. zonatus* (zebra plant) is also striking, the leaves being horizontally banded grey and bronzy green, up to 9in(23cm) long.

CTENANTHE
One of the most striking of foliage plants, *C.*

oppenheimiana 'Tricolor' (never-never plant) is a tufted perennial. The leaves are boldly marked in herring bone fashion creamy-green and dark green with splashes of cream above and red undersides. May eventually grow 3-6ft(1-1.8m) tall. Keep in a warm and humid place shaded from direct sun. Grow in pots of a peat-based mix to which has been added ⅓ part of grit or coarse sharp sand. Repot and increase by division in spring.

DENDROBIUM
Of the many dendrobiums in cultivation, most of which thrive in cooler temperatures, one of the commonest and most popular, *D. bigibbum phalaenopsis (D. phalaenopsis)*, is a tropical orchid needing warmth and humidity. It has large, stem-like pseudobulbs and flowers up to 3½in(9cm) across in shades of rose, lilac and purple with a deeper throat, stems 1ft(30cm) long. Grow in a mix of ⅓-½ sphagnum moss and ½-⅔ osmunda or tree fern fibre. Repot after flowering or when new roots appear and increase by division at the same time.

DRACAENA
Splendid foliage plants for growing indoors with leaves boldly striped and marked, most dracaenas will survive a minimum temperature of around 55°F(13°C) but need warmth and humidity generally. Shade from sun in summer. They will grow in peat- or loam-based mixes and should be repotted in spring. Increase by seed in spring, cuttings spring to summer. *D. deremensis* has green leaves up to 1½ft(45cm) long, the variety 'Bausei' shorter leaves slow growing to about 16ft(5m); with a white central stripe. *D. fragrans* 'Massangeana' has broad leaves with a central yellow stripe, may reach 20ft(6m) in time. *D. marginata*, narrow green leaves with red margins and centre stripe, to 7ft(2m). *D. sanderiana*, narrow grey-green leaves with cream margins, to 7ft(2m).

EPIDENDRUM (buttonhole orchid)
These interesting orchids vary greatly in flower shape and colour – not always large but often brilliantly coloured. They require humid, warm conditions and should be grown in orchid pots or baskets with a ⅔ osmunda fibre and ⅓ sphagnum moss mix. Keep

shaded from strong spring and summer sun. Divide in spring or summer if needed. Many different epidendrums are available and only a few can be mentioned here. *E. ciliare* has remarkable flowers with long pale green petals and a fringed pale blue to white lip on 10in(25cm) stems. *E. cochleatum* (cockle shell orchid) flowers with pale green petals and a yellow rayed purple-black lip shaped like a cockle shell and each flower upside down due to twisted stems themselves on stems 1-1½ft(30-45cm) long. *E. ibaguense (E. radicans)*, flowers red, orange or yellow. *E. stamfordianum*, yellow and white flowers with purple-red spots, fragrant, leafy stems to 3ft(90cm).

EUPHORBIA (spurge)
The shrubby spurges need warmth, humidity and yet good ventilation in summer. This is especially true of the popular poinsettia which is unlikely to produce its best colour otherwise. Grow them in loam- or peat-based mixes and place the pots in a well lit position. When they have finished flowering keep them nearly dry. In spring cut the stems down to 4-6in(10-15cm) and a week later begin watering again. Once growth starts the plants may be repotted and cuttings taken. *E. fulgens* (scarlet plume) a lovely shrub to 4-6ft(1.2-1.8m) and may be smothered, along the arching branches, with the orange-scarlet flowers; can be raised as an annual from cuttings taken every spring. *E. milii (E. splendens* crown of thorns) grows to 1-2ft(30-60cm) has spiny stems and brilliant red flowers. *E. pulcherrima* (poinsettia, Christmas star), is now available with flowers in red, scarlet, pink and white on compact bushes.

FICUS (fig)
Attractive evergreen foliage plants of diverse habit, figs do best in warmth, humidity and some shade in summer. Grow in peat-based mix in pots or hanging baskets according to species. Feed fortnightly during the summer. Repot in spring. Increase by cuttings in summer. *F. benjamina* (weeping fig) has gracefully drooping branches, eventually a tall tree, up to 6ft(1.8m) tall. *F. elastica* (rubber plant), which grows up to 4ft(1.2m) has several popular varieties: 'Decora', broad glossy green leaves, reddish underneath and 10in(25cm) or more long, eventually a tree; 'Doescheri', leaves variegated green, grey and white, sometimes pink flushed; 'Variegata', green variegated cream leaves. *F. pumila* (climbing fig) tolerates cooler conditions, small leaves, climbs to 5ft(1.5m) if supported or will trail, when it is considerably smaller. *F. sagittata (F. radicans* rooting fig) trailing stems, small lance-shaped leaves, good for hanging baskets, especially in the variety 'Variegata' with grey-green and cream leaves; height 3-4in(8-10cm).

GARDENIA
A beautiful evergreen shrub, *G. jasminoides* (cape jasmine), is grown for its lovely white fragrant flowers, and may reach 6ft(1.8m), but usually less in pots. Grow in pots of a peat-based mix, in a warm humid environment. Shade from strong sun. Feed fortnightly in summer. Repot and take cuttings in spring. Cut back plants after flowering to ensure bushiness. The variety 'Fortuniana' has double white flowers which turn cream.

GUZMANIA
Guzmanias have fine rosettes of leaves, usually of a deep green, with brilliantly coloured centres. Warmth, humidity but shade from strong summer sun are needed. Grow in a peat-based mix mixed with 50% sphagnum moss. Keep the centre of the rosettes filled with water except in winter. Repot and increase by offsets in spring and summer. *G. lingulata*, has narrow leaves to 1½ft(45cm) long and a bright red flower stem, about 1ft(30cm) tall, which persists for many weeks. *G. sanguinea*, has leaves of about 1ft(30cm) long the central ones being bright scarlet when the plant flowers, the small flowers are yellow to white.

HOWEA (sentry palm)
Howeas with their graceful arching fronds are attractive plants for large pots or tubs. Although large trees in the wild they are likely to be less than 9-10ft(2.7-3m) indoors. Keep warm and humid, and grow them in a loam-based mix. Keep well-watered when growing, from spring to autumn, then gradually reduce until they are allowed to nearly dry out before watering again. Feed fortnightly in summer. Repot in spring and propagate by seed then. *H. belmoreana (Kentia belmoreana*, curly palm) has upward-pointing

leaflets on arching fronds. *H. forsterana (Kentia forsterana* sentry or thatch leaf palm) has horizontal or drooping leaflets on more upright fronds.

HYMENOCALLIS (spider lily)
Beautiful white-flowered bulbs but not always easy to obtain, there are several species and hybrids two of which are described here. The lovely scented flowers have slender petals surrounding a trumpet borne on a stout stem. The strap-shaped leaves are long and arching. Grow in a humid atmosphere with warmth but lightly shaded from strong sun in summer. Keep well-watered when in leaf, and feed fortnightly when growing, but only just moist otherwise. Grow in loam-based mix with the bulb not quite covered. Repot from late autumn to spring and increase by removing offsets at the same time. *H. littoralis (H. americana)* has leaves which may grow 2½-3ft(75-90cm) long and clusters of large flowers. *H. narcissiflora (Ismene calathina* Peruvian daffodil) has 2ft(60cm) leaves and large flowers with green-flushed throats.

HYPOCYRTA (pouch flower)
The unusual pouch-shaped, orange and red flowers of *H. glabra* are set off well by the dark green, glossy leaves of this small, 9in(25cm) high, shrubby plant. Keep warm and humid but shaded lightly in summer. Grow in a peat-based mix. Cut flowered stems back to keep the plants bushy. Propagate by soft cuttings in summer.

IRESINE
Attractive plants with strongly coloured foliage for growing indoors but which may also be bedded out in the summer. Grow in loam-based mix kept practically dry in winter. Remove the uninteresting flower spikes to help keep the plants bushy. Repot and take cuttings in spring; plants bedded out should be potted in autumn. *I. herbstii* (beefsteak plant) maroon red leaves with yellowish veins but green with yellow veins in the variety 'Aureo-reticulata', to 1½ft(45cm) or more tall. *I. lindenii* (bloodleaf) has deep blood-red leaves or yellow with green markings in the variety 'Formosa', about 2ft(60cm) tall.

KOHLERIA (tree gloxinia)
A group of herbaceous plants and shrubs with bright tubular flowers. Keep them warm and humid and grow them in loam-based mix. Increase herbaceous plants by division in spring, shrubs by cuttings in summer. *K. amabilis (Isoloma amabile)* a herbaceous plant with deep rose flowers, spotted purple-red over dark green leaves and growing to 2ft(60cm). *K. eriantha (Isoloma erianthum)* is a shrub with yellow-spotted red flowers, flowering when young but eventually reaching about 4ft(1.2m).

LAELIA
Lovely orchids for warm and humid conditions. Grow in orchid pots or baskets filled with mixed ⅔ osmunda fibre and ⅓ sphagnum moss. Shade from strong spring and summer sun. Divide in spring or summer to increase. *L. anceps*, small egg-like pseudobulbs each growing a single leaf, flowers 4in(10cm) across of rosy-lilac with a yellow-striped, purple-margined lip; many forms are grown with different coloured flowers. *L. purpurata*, has large pseudobulbs about 1½ft(45cm) long, single leaved, flowers scented and large, to 8in(20cm) wide, white- to pink-petalled and with an attractive yellow-throated, purple lip.

MANDEVILLA
Splendidly flowered climbing plants needing large containers or an indoor border for success. Keep warm but well ventilated yet humid if possible and shade from strong sun. Grow in a loam-based mix and feed every fortnight during the summer. Increase by cuttings in summer, seed in spring. *M. laxa (M. suaveolens* Chilean jasmine) beautiful large, fragrant white lily-like flowers and heart shaped leaves, to 16ft(5m), best in a border. *M. splendens (Dipladenia splendens)*, fine, large pink flowers, elliptic leaves, to 10ft(3m), cut back hard during the winter.

MEDINILLA
A remarkable plant, *M. magnifica*, is an evergreen shrub with magnificent, drooping clusters of flowers in shades of pink, and large leaves. It needs warmth and humidity, large pots or tubs filled with a peat-based mix and plenty of moisture. Take care not to overwater and rot the plant however. It may grow to between 3-7ft(90-210cm). Increase by cuttings taken in spring.

MIMOSA

Not the mimosa of the flower shop, which comes from the tree *Acacia dealbata*, but a small shrubby perennial *M. pudica* (sensitive or humble plant) which grows to about 3ft(90cm). The great attraction of it is that when touched the leaflets fold together, and hence its common names. Even without this attribute it makes an attractive foliage plant with its graceful leaves. It is usually grown as an annual. Grow it in any good commercial mix. Sow seed in spring.

MUSA (banana)

Most of the bananas of commerce grow on plants too large for the home but there are a few shorter varieties which make attractive plants for large containers. They have the typical banana foliage fronds. Give them warmth, humidity and in summer light shade. Grow them in a loam-based mix. Repot late spring to early summer when they may be increased by offsets, or increase by seed in spring. *M. acuminata* 'Dwarf Cavendish' (Canary Island or Chinese banana) grows to 7-8ft(2.1-2.4m). *M. coccinea* (scarlet banana) has scarlet flower parts and grows to 3-5ft(90-150cm).

NEOREGELIA 4

Some species of neoregelia are among the most brightly coloured bromeliads. They form rosettes of leaves, the centre of which should be kept filled with water. Grow in small pots of peat-based mix kept just moist. The plant usually dies after flowering but will have sent up new shoots which may be detached and grown on. *N. carolinae* (*N. marechalii* blushing bromeliad) the centre of the rosette turns red contrasting with the deep green leaves up to 16in(40cm) long, or, in the variety 'Tricolor' with leaves striped cream and sometimes pink flushed. *N. spectabilis* (fingernail plant) has red-tipped leaves.

NIDULARIUM

Beautifully coloured bromeliads, nidulariums form rosettes of leaves which should be kept filled with water. Grow them in small pots of a peat-based mix kept just moist. After flowering the plant usually dies but should have sent up new shoots which may be detached and grown on. *N. fulgens* (*N. pictum* blushing bromeliad) the 1ft(30cm) long green leaves

are spotted with a darker green, the centre turning bright red. *N. innocentii*, green flushed purple 1ft(30cm) long leaves, centre red but in the variety 'Lineatum' the green leaves are striped white with a red and green centre.

ONCIDIUM (dancing lady orchid)

Lovely orchids with flowers of many different shapes and colours. Grow them in orchid pots or baskets filled with a mix of ⅓ sphagnum moss and ⅔ osmunda fibre. Shade from sun in spring and summer but otherwise keep in full light. Divide in spring or summer if needed. *O. flexuosum* (dancing doll orchid) masses of small, brown-barred yellow flowers dance on flower heads 2-3ft(60-90cm) long. *O. papilio* (butterfly orchid) amazing flowers, the three upper long and reddish, the lower ones barred red and yellow on stems 2-4ft(60-120cm) long.

PAPHIOPEDILUM (lady's slipper)

Large-flowered orchids, the flowers typically having one upright petal, two wing petals and a lower petal or lip which is rather slipper- or pouch-shaped, the different types of petal are usually of different colours or markings. They have strap-shaped leaves and no pseudobulbs. Keep humid from spring to autumn and shade from sun. Grow in pots of equal parts of sphagnum moss, osmunda fibre and loam kept just moist. Feed fortnightly with half strength liquid fertilizer when the plants are in growth. Repot and increase plants by division then, in spring. *P. callosum*, white, green and purple veined, green, rose and red-brown flowers, stem 1ft(30cm), leaves spotted blackish. *P. insigne*, yellowish green, brownish-red spotted veins, greenish-yellow and brown suffused flowers, stem 1ft(30cm). Many other varieties are available.

PEPEROMIA (radiator plant)

Good house plants with attractive leaves, peperomias need warmth and humidity but shade from strong sun. Grow in pots of commercial mixes mixed with ⅓ sphagnum moss if possible, kept moist except in winter when let it become nearly dry. Repot spring or summer annually when plants may be increased by division or cuttings also. *P. argyreia* (*P. sandersii* watermelon peperomia) green leaves with silver-grey

1 *Adiantum tenerum* (brittle maidenhair)
3 *Columnea* × *banksii*
5 *Ruellia macrantha* (Christmas pride)

2 *Calathea zebrina* (zebra plant)
4 *Neoregelia carolinae* 'Tricolor'
6 *Sinningia speciosa* vars (gloxinias)

between the veins on a compact plant up to 10in(25cm) in height. *P. caperata* (emerald ripple peperomia) dark green leaves with sunken veins, compact to 6in(15cm) high. *P. magnoliifolia* has large leaves, 4-6in(10-15cm) glossy green or in the variety 'Variegata' cream becoming variegated with green and all over green, on a 10in(25cm) or more tall plant. *P. obtusifolia* (baby rubber plant) leaves green on a compact plant to 6in(15cm) high, but the leaves bordered cream and with a greyish-green centre in the variety 'Variegata'.

PHALAENOPSIS (moth orchid)
Beautifully flowered orchids without a pseudobulb but with thick stems which carry a few leaves. Keep warm, humid but lightly shaded. Grow in baskets of osmunda fibre or fibre and sphagnum moss, kept moist at all times. Feed occasionally from spring to autumn. Repot only when essential as root disturbance is resented and increase by division at the same time if needed. Increase also by plantlets which sometimes form on flowering stems. *P. amabilis*, white petals give an almost rounded appearance to the flowers with yellow in the centre marked red, flower stem to 2ft(60cm), leaves to 10in(25cm) long. *P. lueddemanniana*, fragrant, white/purple/magenta barred flowers, flower stem 1ft(30cm) pale green leaves 1ft(30cm) long.

PLUMBAGO (leadwort)
A beautiful plant when covered with its deep rosy-red flowers, *P. indica* (*P. rosea* scarlet leadwort) is a semi-climbing shrub which may be trained to a 2-3ft(60-90cm) bush. An evergreen with leaves to about 4in(10cm) long. To keep it bushy, cut the plant back every spring to 6in(15cm). Grow in pots of loam-based compost and feed every fortnight in summer, keep drier in winter. Increase by cuttings when cut back.

RHIPSALIDOPSIS
Splendid, easily grown and flowered, epiphytic cacti which, though doing well at lower temperatures will thrive at 60°F(16°C). They produce long flat jointed stems, rather leaf-like and from which the flowers arise. Grow in pots of a rhododendron potting mix or one where lime is at a minimum. Keep moist allowing

the soil to nearly dry out between each watering, and feed fortnightly during the summer. Pot or repot spring. Increase by cuttings, using two or three joints per cutting and two or three cuttings per pot, in summer. *R. gaertneri* (*Schlumbergera gaertneri* Easter cactus) bright red flowers, stem joints 2-3in(5-7.5cm) long, up to 1ft(30cm) high. *R. rosea*, scented pink flowers, stem joints 1-1½in(2.5-4cm) long, plant to 6in(15cm) high.

RUELLIA 5
Fine evergreen plants with attractive flowers and leaves, the flowers produced in winter. Grow in warmth and pots of peat-based mix. Shade from direct sun. Repot and increase by cuttings or seed in spring. *R. macrantha* (Christmas pride) large pink trumpet flowers, a shrub to 6ft(1.8m) unless cut back. *R. portellae*, purplish-pink flowers, an annual or perennial plant 10-12in(25-30cm) tall.

SANSEVIERIA (bowstring hemp)
A very popular indoor plant, *S. trifasciata* (mother-in-law's tongue, snake plant) does best in some warmth though often confined to cooler regions. The stiff leaves are banded light, dark and silvery green and grow 2-4ft(60-120cm) tall but in the variety 'Laurentii' they also have yellow margins. The variety 'Hahnii' has short leaves, sometimes up to 1ft(30cm) long, forming rosettes. Grow in any commercial mix kept moist but do not overwater. Feed every fortnight when growing. Bowstring hemps are very slow growing and repotting is generally unnecessary until tightly pot-bound. This can be done in spring, at which time plants may be increased by division.

SCHEFFLERA (umbrella tree)
Foliage plants requiring plenty of room but often slow growing, doing best in some warmth and humidity. Grow in any commercial mix kept moist but less so in winter. Feed fortnightly in summer. Repot in spring. Increase by cuttings in summer or seed in spring. *S. actinophylla* (*Brassaia actinophylla* Australian umbrella tree) numerous leaflets radiating from an off centre stem, leaflets up to 1ft(30cm) long, shrub to 8ft(2.4m) in pots or tubs. *S. digitata*, leaflets seven or more radiating from a central stem, shrub to 7ft(2.1m) in pots or tubs.

SCHLUMBERGERA

Excellent winter flowering epiphytic cacti which do best in warmth but are often grown with some success at lower temperatures. The long flat jointed stems are rather leaf-like and give rise to the flowers. Grow in pots of rhododendron mix or one with little lime. Keep moist but let the soil nearly dry out between each watering, and feed fortnightly during the summer. Pot or repot spring. Increase by cuttings in summer using two to three joints per cutting and two to three cuttings per pot. *S.* × *buckleyi* (*S. bridgesii* Christmas cactus) often sold under the name of the next species, cerise to magenta flowers, stem joints ¾-2in(2-5cm) long, arching, stems 1ft(30cm) or more long. *S. truncata* (*Zygocactus truncatus* crab cactus) similar to the Christmas cactus but the stem joints are toothed and it is earlier flowering.

SCINDAPSUS

Decorative foliage climbers for warm conditions which may grow to 40ft(12m) in the wild but less under cultivation. Keep humid and shaded from sun in summer. Grow in pots of peat-based mix. Keep moist but not overwatered. Provide support, such as a moss-covered stick. Repot in spring and increase by cuttings in summer. *S. aureus* (*Epipremnum aureum* pothos, devil's ivy) shiny leaves, bright green irregularly marked and marbled yellow, up to 10ft(3m) in pot; the variety 'Marble Queen' has white to cream leaves marked with green and grey green. *S. pictus* has dark green leaves marked with grey-green, to 8ft(2.4m) in pots; the variety 'Argyraeus' has leaves marked with silvery-grey spots.

SINNINGIA (gloxinia) 6

Showy plants, splendid in flower and leaf, the modern strains of *S. speciosa* are not difficult indoor plants. Keep warm and shade from strong sun. Grow in a peat-based mix kept moist while the plants are in growth but take care not to overwater or splash leaves which mark. After flowering when the leaves start to yellow gradually dry the tubers off and store them at about 55°F(13°C); first year sown plants will probably not die down and should be grown on into the next year. Replant tubers in spring. Increase by cutting tubers, which have started into growth, into pieces with a shoot, and by seed. Tubers should be

planted with the upper surface level with the soil. Established plants (roots filling their pots) should be fed fortnightly. The choice of sinningias is now very wide and new strains are regularly offered, some are dwarf at about 6in(15cm) and others may be twice that. Flowers are available in self colours, picotee, or spotted and marked in various ways in rich blue, voilet, pink, red as well as white; some double-flowered hybrids are also becoming available.

SMITHIANTHA (*Naegelia* temple bells)

Lovely plants with rather foxglove-like flowers in brighter colours and with velvety leaves. Keep them warm 60°F(16°C), moist and humid while they are growing and flowering. After flowering, when the plants have died down store the dry, dormant rhizomes at about 54°F(12°C). Repot in spring when the rhizomes may be divided, and use a peat-based mix. *S. cinnabarina*, bright red flowers banded yellow to white inside, deep green, red to purple flushed leaves, up to 2ft(60cm). *S. zebrina*, scarlet flowers, yellow-banded below, throat yellow with scarlet spots, leaves deep green with purplish-brown veins, to 2½ft(45cm). Hybrids, sometimes listed under *S.* × *hybrida*, in a wide flower colour range, and of variable size are available and include 'Carmel', white flowers spotted red, leaves reddish flushed; 'Elke', gold flowers, olive leaves; 'Orange King', deep orange flowers, bronze leaves.

SPATHIPHYLLUM (spathe flower)

There are several species and hybrids all rather similar with scented white arum-like flowers, and dark, evergreen leaves, differing mainly in height and size of parts. Keep warm and humid. Grow preferably in loam-based mix kept moist. Shade from summer sun, but feed plants fortnightly then. Repot spring and increase by division then. *S.* × 'Clevelandii' (white anthurium) large spathes, leaf blades large, to 2ft(60cm). *S.* × 'Mauna Loa', large spathes and leaves, plant 1½-2ft(45-60cm). *S. wallisii* (white sails) smaller spathes and leaves, 10-12in(25-30cm) tall.

STEPHANOTIS

Very fragrant white flowers are borne by the climbing *S. floribunda* (Madagascar jasmine) which may grow

10ft(3m) or more, pot grown. Deep evergreen, oval leaves. Keep warm and grow in pots of loam-based mix, watered well in summer and fed fortnightly then; keep compost just moist over winter. Repot in spring and at the same time cut back straggly growth. Increase by cuttings in summer.

TIBOUCHINA
Rich violet to purple flowers with dark sickle-shaped stamens decorate *T. urvilleana* (*T. semidecandra* glory bush). The flowers are about 4in(10cm) across and the shrub may in very favourable circumstances reach 15ft(4.6m). Grow in large pots or tubs of loam-based mix or in an indoor border. Keep warm and water well while growing, feed fortnightly spring to autumn. Cut plants back if required in winter or spring. Repot spring. Increase by cuttings in spring or summer.

TILLANDSIA
The two bromeliads described here are very different in appearance but both require warmth, humidity and shading from strong sun. *T. flabellata* forms a dense rosette of leaves, has a branched reddish flower stem and reddish flowers with violet-blue petals. Grow in small pots of equal parts of sand and of a peat-based mixture, keep moist and feed fortnightly in summer. Repot in spring. Increase by offsets in summer. *T. usneoides* (Spanish moss) is a curious plant with thread-like grey-green leaves about 2in(5cm) long on wiry 3ft(90cm) long stems under indoor conditions but much more in the wild; rootless, the plant drapes over other plant branches. Moisture and food are absorbed through the leaves which should be sprayed daily and fed with a foliar fertilizer during the summer. Increase by removing pieces of stem.

List 2 Plants for slightly heated conservatories, extensions and living rooms
Here, plants and people have equal importance. The level of humidity is less than that of List 1, and the temperature is usually kept above 50°F (10°C).

ABUTILON (flowering maple)
Shrubby evergreens with maple-like leaves and attractive pendulous flowers. Grow in large pots or tubs or an indoor border. In containers growth is restricted up to about 4ft(1.2m) otherwise they grow up to 8ft(2.4m). Most commercial mixes are suitable for containers. Keep moist and ventilate in summer. Repot in spring when cuttings may also be taken for annually grown plants or to increase stock. *A. × hybridum*, has many named varieties including 'Ashford Red' with crimson flowers, 'Canary Bird' yellow turning reddish, 'Savitzii' red veined orange, leaves variegated with white, a smaller plant. *A. pictum* (*A. striatum*) 'Thompsonii' deep orange, red-veined flowers, dark green leaves variegated creamy yellow.

AGAVE (century plant)   7
Though grown mainly for their attractive rosettes of leaves, agaves often have spectacularly tall flower stems, not produced usually in small containers. Grow in large pots or tubs of any free-draining mix kept moist from spring to autumn but much drier in winter. Keep well ventilated in warm, dry weather. Repot in spring. Increase by offsets when repotting. *A. americana* (century plant) leaves up to 3ft(90cm) long, toothy, grey green, flower stem to 20ft(6m) or more; the variety 'Marginata' has yellowish margins to the leaves, and 'Mediopicta' leaves with a broad central yellow stripe. *A. filifera* (thread agave) has a dense rosette of leaves 10-12in(25-30cm) long, the green edged with hard white growth which disbands into threads, flower stem 6ft(1.8m) or more.

ALOE
The leaves usually forming rosettes for which they are grown, aloes are nevertheless of many forms. The flowers are usually of some shade of reddish-orange borne on long stems well clear of the foliage. Grow in any free-draining potting mix, if necessary adding

sharp sand or grit. Keep moist at all times, ventilated and in full light. Repot in spring and increase by offsets at the same time. *A. aristata* (torch plant) stemless, dense rosettes of 4in(10cm) long leaves, flowers orange-red on 1ft(30cm) stems. *A. ferox* (cape aloe) stem eventually 6ft(1.8m) or more but slow growing, leaves up to 3ft(90cm) long in a dense rosette, flowers reddish on stems 3-4ft(90-120cm) tall. *A. variegata* (partridge-breasted aloe) stem up to 6in(15cm) formed as lower leaves die off, leaves triangular in section 4-6in(10-15cm) long, green banded with white spots, warm pink flowers on 1ft(30cm) stems.

APHELANDRA

The zebra plant or saffron spike, *A. squarrosa*, has attractively cream-veined green leaves and yellow pyramids of flowers from late summer to winter. Plants may grow to 4ft(1.2m). Shade from sun but grow them in a warm, humid atmosphere and pots of any commercial mix. Repot and take cuttings in spring. Cut the stems back after flowering to a pair of leaves to keep the plants bushy. The variety 'Louisae' is more compact.

APOROCACTUS

The long trailing stems and rich pink flowers make *A. flagelliformis* (rat's-tail cactus) a splendid, free flowering plant for hanging baskets. Stems to 15in(38cm) long, spiny. Grow in peat-based mix, in pots or baskets, kept moist and feed fortnightly during the summer. Repot in spring. Increase by cuttings in summer.

ARAUCARIA

The soft, light green leaves of young plants make *A. heterophylla* (Norfolk Island pine) a delightful and graceful plant. As a pot plant it is slow growing, only growing to 4-6ft(1.2-1.8m) in several years though in the wild it may reach 200ft(60m) eventually. Grow in pots or tubs of a commercial mix, taking care not to overwater. Ventilate and shade from summer sun. Increase by seed sown in spring or autumn.

ARDISIA

Though it does have scented, small white to reddish flowers *A. crispa* (*A. crenata* coralberry) is grown more for its bright coral-red fruit. A graceful shrub to 4ft(1.2m) or more the fruit appears in winter and lasts for many months. Grow in pots of commercial mix. Shade from hot sun. Repot in spring and increase by cuttings or seed then.

ASCLEPIAS (milkweed)

Many milkweeds are hardy but *A. curassavica* (bloodflower) needs some warmth to produce its brilliant orange flowers. A shrubby plant growing to 3ft(90cm) or more it may be kept in check by cutting it back in spring. Grow in a peat-based mix kept moist. Repot and increase by seed in spring. The variety 'Aurea' has orange-yellow flowers.

ASPARAGUS

The delicate, feathery foliage makes these plants attractive – the flowers, though scented, are inconspicuous. Grow in a commercial mix kept moist and do not overwater. Keep out of full sun in summer. Repot in spring and increase by division at the same time. *A. densiflorus* 'Sprengeri' (*A. sprengeri* emerald fern) has drooping branches up to 3ft(90cm) long. *A. setaceus* (*A. plumosus* asparagus fern) eventually a climber to 10ft(3m) or more but young plants are non climbing, the variety 'Nanus' remaining dwarf.

ASPIDISTRA

One of the most tolerant of all indoor plants, *A. elatior* (*A. lurida* barroom or cast-iron plant) is grown for its clumps of long arching leaves, dark green or in the variety 'Variegata' green with white stripes. It grows up to 2½ft(75cm) tall. Grow in peat-based mix kept moist but not overwatered, in pots shaded from strong sun. Increase by division in spring.

ASPLENIUM (spleenwort)

Attractive ferns with glossy green fronds. Grow in peat-based mix, in warm, humid situations but shaded from strong sun. Repot and increase by division in spring. *A. bulbiferum* (hen and chicken fern) has finely dissected fronds 2-4ft(60-120cm) long. Plantlets form along the fronds, weighing them down, which may be detached and grown. *A. nidus* (*A. nidus-avis* bird's nest fern) has rather upright fronds forming a rosette shaped like a shuttlecock. The fronds are not divided, to 2-4ft(60-120cm) long.

ASTROPHYTUM (star cactus)
Cacti with short cylindrical or globular bodies, some with attractive ribbing, and bright flowers. Grow in a loam-based mix with an equal amount of grit or coarse sharp sand. Repot in spring. Increase by seed sown in spring. *A. capricorne* (goat's-horn cactus) globular when young but elongating with age, up to 8in(20cm). It has eight ribs studded with white star-like scales and twisted brown spines. *A. ornatum* (star cactus), short cylindrical body when young elongating to 1ft(30cm). Ribs eight, whitish spotted and with yellowish-brown spines.

BEGONIA
There are too many attractive begonias which may be grown indoors to mention more than a selection here. Some are grown for their foliage alone, some for their brilliant flowers, some for both reasons and they may be tuberous or fibrous rooted, or grow from rhizomes. Grow them in a peat-based mix. Shade from sun in summer but feed fortnightly then. Propagate all kinds by leaf and stem cuttings spring to summer, tuberous and rhizomatous rooted species in spring, or by seed in early spring. *B. boweri* (eyelash begonia) light green leaves, wavy margined and with dark brown blotches. Pale pink to white flowers. To 9in(23cm) tall. *B. coccinea* (angelwing begonia) shrubby with bamboo-like stems 3-6ft/90-180cm. Red-edged glossy green leaves and drooping bunches of coral-pink flowers. *B. masoniana* (iron-cross begonia) puckered green leaves boldly marked with a brownish cross. Grows to about 8in(20cm) from rhizomes. *B. semperflorens* (wax begonia) available in many strains with white, red, pink and orange flowers, usually green leaves but some with shiny brown foliage. Densely bushy, from fibrous roots, 4-18in(10-45cm) tall. *B. × tuberhybrida*, has several differing groups of brightly flowered plants from tubers. The groups include the Camellia flowered with strong, upright stems, the Multiflora group is similar but shorter, while the Pendula group has arching, drooping stems. Strong plants may grow to 2ft(60cm) but many of the cultivars are much smaller.

BILLBERGIA (vase plant)
Attractive plants which form rosettes of leaves from which grow the gracefully drooping flowers on arching stems. Easy to grow in peat-based mixes they should be kept warm but shaded from direct sun. Repot when needed in spring or summer when the plants may also be increased by division. Feed with liquid fertilizer every month when the plants fill their pots. *B. nutans* (queen's or angel's tears) greenish yellow, purple-margined flowers from pink stalks, about 1½ft(45cm) high. *B. pyramidalis* (foolproof plant or summer torch) has spikes of crimson, purple-tipped flowers from red stems, 12-15in(30-38cm).

BOUGAINVILLEA 8
Beautifully flowered climbers, the varieties of *B. × buttiana* have blooms in shades of crimson, magenta, red, pink and orange to yellow. Grown in large pots they will reach 5-8ft(1.5-2.4m), while in indoor borders they will achieve 20ft(6m) or more. In containers use a loam-based mix. Keep plants well ventilated in warm weather and watered; keep drier overwinter. In small pots pinch back plants to keep them bushier. Increase by cuttings in summer.

BOUVARDIA
Easily grown and attractive shrubs, bouvardias have flowers in shades of red and pink. Keep them warm but shaded from strong sun. Grow them in a loam-based, rich mix. They will require plenty of water when growing well. Young plants should have their shoot tips pinched out to make bushier plants. In winter keep the plants drier after they have finished flowering. Repot if needed in spring when cuttings may also be taken. *B. × domestica* is a name covering a group of hybrids up to 2ft(60cm) high, including 'Mary' with pale pink flowers, 'President Cleveland' has bright crimson-scarlet flowers, and 'Rosea' with rose-salmon flowers. *B. ternifolia* (*B. triphylla*) (scarlet trompetilla) carries its brilliant scarlet flowers from summer through autumn into winter, and grows up to 6ft(1.8m).

BRUNFELSIA
The lovely flowers of *B. pauciflora* appear through most of the year but are best in summer and autumn, blue purple and up to 3in(7.5cm) across in the variety 'Macrantha'. Known as Yesterday, today and tomorrow, the plant is usually offered as *B. calycina*. Evergreen, it grows 3ft(90cm) or more. Grow in pots

of peat-based mix and shade from direct, hot sun. Repot in spring. Increase by cuttings in spring.

CALCEOLARIA (slipperwort)

Modern, large-flowered hybrids of C. × *herbeohybrida*, have brilliant blooms in shades of yellow, orange, pink, red and crimson, marked and spotted in a variety of ways. Grow in pots of loam-based mix, annually from seed sown in late spring or early summer. They grow from about 6-18in(15-45cm) tall according to variety.

CALLISTEMON (bottlebrush) 9

Lovely evergreen shrubs with flowers in bottlebrush formed spikes of flower, mainly in shades of red. Grow in large pots or tubs or an indoor border. Use a lime-free mix if possible. Keep well ventilated but in a sunny position. Repot in spring and increase by seed sown then or by cuttings in summer. C. *citrinus* (crimson bottlebrush) has crimson flowers and may grow to 20ft(6m). C. *speciosus* (Albany bottlebrush) has scarlet flowers, grows up to 10ft(3m) and is an excellent indoor shrub.

CESTRUM

Freely borne clusters of flowers are the great attraction of these plants which may be grown as shrubs or climbers. Grow in large pots or containers of any commercial mix or in an indoor border and support them with wire or stakes. Shade from hot summer sun, and keep well ventilated in summer. If space is limited cut out three-year-old shoots after flowering in winter, the best flowering usually occurring on two- and three-year-old shoots. Repot in spring and increase by seed sown then or by cuttings in summer. C. *aurantiaca*, orange flowers, semi-evergreen, to 10ft(3m) or more. C. *elegans* (C. *purpureum*), reddish-purple to crimson flowers, evergreen, to 10ft(3m) or more.

CEROPEGIA

A splendid trailing plant, C. *woodii* (string of hearts), is grown for its attractive leaves and curious flowers. The stems are wiry and carry many heart shaped leaves, green and silver marbled on top, purple below; deep purple flowers which turn upright from their swollen bases with a curiously formed tube. The stems may trail to 6ft(1.8m) and also have, every so often, small tubers developing along their length and from which new plants may be raised. Grow in hanging baskets or pots from which the stems may trail of half and half peat-based mix and coarse sharp sand, half burying the tubers. Keep watered but only just moist in winter and in a sunny position. Repot in spring and increase by tubers or seed then.

CHLOROPHYTUM

An easily grown foliage plant, C. *comosum* (the spider plant) is probably best known in its variegated form C. *comosum* 'Vittatum' (C. *elatum variegatum*), the green leaves striped centrally with white. Both have long gracefully arching leaves and form clumps, about 10in(25cm) high, from which long trailing flower stems arise. Besides bearing flowers small plantlets are also developed and from which yet further stems bearing further plantlets develop and so on and eventually the stem may reach up to 6ft(1.8m) long with several branches. Grow in baskets or pots from which the stems may trail, of any commercial mix. Repot spring to autumn and increase by division at the same time or by detaching plantlets with several leaves and potting them.

CISSUS

The tolerance of C. *antarctica* (kangaroo vine) makes it a justifiably popular foliage plant. The tough, saw edged leaves cover a plant which may reach 15ft(4.5m) or more but usually less. Grow in any commercial mix and provide support. Repot in spring. Increase by cuttings in summer.

CITRUS

There are two very good citrus species which may be grown fairly easily, and without taking up too much space indoors. They are evergreen shrubs. Grow in any commercial mix. Keep moist but never over-watered, shade lightly in summer and keep well ventilated. Repot in spring but increase by cuttings with a heel in summer. C. *limon* 'Meyer', a dwarf lemon to about 4ft(1.2m) with fragrant, purple-tinted white flowers, followed, in favourable conditions by smooth, thick-skinned lemons which take about a year to ripen. C. *mitis* (Calamondin orange) is now known as a hybrid between C. *reticulata*, mandarin orange, and the kumquat genus *Fortunella*, × *Citrofortunella mitis* being its new name. It is a small bushy shrub, up to 5ft(1.5m) with lightly scented white flowers followed by small oranges.

CLIANTHUS
The easiest clianthus, *C. puniceus* (glory pea or parrot's bill), is an attractive shrubby plant with brilliant red flowers set off against feathery evergreen foliage. As an indoor plant it will grow 6-12ft(1.8-3.6m). Grow in an indoor border or pots of a loam-based mix. A good tub plant. Give plenty of ventilation. Repot spring and increase by seed then or in late summer by cuttings with a heel.

CLIVIA (Kaffir lily)
The long-flowering period, from spring to autumn, makes *C. miniata* a splendid pot plant. The flowers are yellow-throated scarlet, erect and in clusters of 10-20. The dark green leaves, about 1½ft(45cm) long, arch over. Grow in pots of commercial mix well watered in summer but almost dry in winter. Repot only when necessary in spring or after flowering when plants may also be increased by division. Feed fortnightly in summer.

CODIAEUM (croton)
Among the most beautiful of foliage plants, the leaves of *C. variegatum pictum* come in a wide range of shapes and spots, splashes and veins of various colours on plants to 3ft(90cm) or more tall. Plants need warmth and humidity. Grow in any commercial mix and shade from direct sun. Repot in spring and increase by tip cuttings then or in summer.

COLEUS (flame nettle)
Easily grown plants, *C. blumei* has rather nettle-shaped leaves, sometimes frilled, cut or waved at the margins, in a wide range of colours. It is usually grown as an annual though actually a perennial, and restricted to a height of about 1½ft(45cm) or less. Grow in pots of loam-based mix. Shade from direct sun. Pinch out growing tips of young plants several times to create the desired bushiness and feed more established plants fortnightly in summer. Cut down plants to be grown on into the next year to a few pairs of buds in winter and repot the plants into a larger

size pot in spring. Increase by seed in spring or cuttings then and in summer.

CORDYLINE
This is an almost hardy plant which does better with a little warmth and although as a wild plant *C. australis* (cabbage tree) does reach tree-like proportions it is usually a 3-6ft(90-180cm) pot plant. The leaves are long, to 3ft(90cm) and sword shaped, and grow from the top of a thick stem. Usually green the leaves may be tinged with bronze and purple in some varieties. Grow in loam-based mix. Repot in spring and increase then by seed or removing suckers.

CRASSULA
Succulent plants with attractive fleshy leaves, some also having nice flowers. Grow in pots of ⅔ commercial mix to which has been added ⅓ coarse sharp sand. Do not overwater and keep well ventilated in sunny weather. Repot spring and increase by seed then or by division and cuttings then or in summer. *C. arborescens* (silver jade plant) rounded grey-green leaves with red margins, rarely flowers in cultivation, to 3ft(90cm) tall. *C. argentea* (jade tree) oval bright green leaves sometimes red margined, pink flowers in summer, to 10ft(3m) in time. *C. falcata* (*Rochea falcata* airplane plant) grey overlapping sickle-shaped leaves, dense flat heads of bright red flowers in summer, 2-2½ft(60-75cm) tall.

CUPHEA 10
Attractive tubular-flowered herbaceous and shrubby plants. Grow in pots of commercial mix and keep well ventilated in warm weather. Repot in spring and increase by seed then and cuttings then or in summer. Cut spindly growth of established plants well back in spring and pinch out the growing tips of young plants to induce bushiness. *C. ignea* (*C. platycentra* cigar flower) brilliant scarlet flowers with a dark band near the tip and white at the tip, bushy to 1ft(30cm) or more. *C.* × *purpurea* (*C. miniata*), bright vermilion flowers on a shrubby plant to 2ft(60cm); the variety 'Firefly' having cerise flowers on a plant only growing to about 15in(38cm).

CYMBIDIUM
The showy flowers of these clump-forming orchids

has led to a wide range of hybrids derived from many species. They have several arching leaves and the pseudobulbs may be very small. Size is variable, 6-30in(15-75cm). Grow in a mix made of sphagnum moss, osmunda fibre, fibrous loam and coarse sharp sand in equal parts, in pots, and kept moist and fed fortnightly when established. Repot when new growth appears and increase by division then. The hybrids available include plants with flowers in shades of pink, red, yellow, apricot, greenish yellow, blush and white, and often prettily marked, spotted and streaked with another colour; the range is constantly added to.

CYRTOMIUM

A splendid evergreen, *C. falcatum* (holly fern) has arching fronds to 2½ft(75cm) long and with glossy dark green holly-like leaflets. Grow in pots of peat-based mix to which has been added a little extra sharp sand. Shade from strong sun and keep slightly humid in summer if possible. Repot and increase by division in spring.

DATURA (thorn apple)

The annual and perennial plants described here are large and spreading with huge trumpet flowers. Grow in large pots of commercial mix or in an indoor border. Feed, lightly shade and ventilate well in summer. Repot and increase by seed in spring. Shrubby plants may also be increased by cuttings spring to autumn. *D. inoxia* (Indian apple or angel's trumpet), has an annual form and a perennial form both of which may be offered under the name *D. meteloides*. They are spreading plants to about 3ft(90cm) with large leaves up to 10in(25cm) long and scented flowers to 8in(20cm) long. The annual usually has flowers from white to pink, the perennial from white to pale lavender. *D. metel* (horn of plenty) has leaves to 8in(20cm) long, and white, violet or yellow 7in(18cm)-long flowers.

DAVALLIA

Ferns with attractive fronds which derive their common names from the fancied resemblances of their rhizomatous surface roots to animals' feet or to the shapes into which they may be trained. Grow in peat-based mix, in pots or baskets attached to moss-covered supports. Keep moist and partially shaded. Increase in spring by division or cutting rhizome sections. *D. canariensis* (hare's- or deer's-foot fern) fronds rather like chervil but leathery and to 18in(45cm) long, rhizomes with brown, hairy scales. *D. mariesii* (squirrel's-foot or ball fern) is similar but smaller with fronds to 10in(25cm), and hardier.

DIEFFENBACHIA (dumb cane)

Beautiful but poisonous foliage plants, the large leaves splashed and spotted in shades of white to yellow. Grow in pots of peat-based mix and keep plants warm and humid and shaded in summer. Repot in spring. Increase by cuttings of stem sections early summer, about 3in(7.5cm) long. Feed established plants fortnightly in summer. *D. amoena* (giant dumb cane), large dark, glossy green leaves with creamy white feathering to the veins, up to 1½ft(45cm) long on a plant to 6ft(1.8m). *D. maculata* (*D. picta* spotted dumb cane), leaves heavily spotted white so that the veins stand out green, to 10in(25cm) long on a plant to 4ft(1.2m); in the variety 'Rudolph Roehrs' the leaves appear almost all yellow with green veins.

DIZYGOTHECA (false aralia)

When young *D. elegantissima* makes an attractive and graceful pot plant to about 4ft(1.2m) tall though ultimately it may become a small tree. The long-stalked leaves are divided into long double-edged saw-like leaflets and of a dark coppery colour. Grow in a peat-based mix. Shade lightly in summer and provide a slightly humid atmosphere. Repot and increase by seed in spring.

ECHINOCACTUS 11

These cacti have ribbed globular to cylindrical bodies and attractive spines. Grow in a loam-based mix mixed half and half with grit or coarse sharp sand. Keep moist but allow to dry between each watering and grow in a sunny, ventilated position. Repot and increase by seed in spring. *E. grusonii* (golden barrel cactus), the yellow flowers are rare in cultivation, globular slowly growing to about 3ft(90cm) yellowish spines. *E. horizonthalonius* (eagle claws) flowers easily, pink, globular to shortly cylindrical up to 1ft(30cm) yellowish to greyish spines.

7 *Agace filifera* (thread agave)
9 *Callistemon speciosus* (Albany bottlebrush)
11 *Echinocactus grusonii* (golden barrel cactus)

8 *Bougainvillea* × *buttiana* var
10 *Cuphea ignea* (cigar flower)
12 *Gerbera jamesonii* (Barberton daisy)

ECHINOCEREUS (hedgehog cactus)
Branching cacti with brilliant flowers which may be followed by spiny, but otherwise edible fruit. Grow in a loam-based mix mixed half and half with coarse sharp sand. Keep moist, allowing the soil to dry between each watering, and grow in a sunny, ventilated position. Repot and increase by seed in spring and by cuttings in summer. *E. cinerascens*, rosy purple flowers, ribbed stems 8-12in(20-30cm) long, small spines. *E. pectinatus*, rosy-magenta flowers, ribbed stems up to 1ft(30cm) but usually much less, small spines; in the variety *rigidissimus* (rainbow cactus) the spines hide the ribs and are in bands of colour around the stem, shades of reddish, pinkish, browny or white spines.

EPIPHYLLUM (orchid cactus)
Grown mainly for the brilliant flowers of the hybrids, in a range of dazzling colours and up to 8in(20cm) across, and also one species as a foliage plant. The flattened stems (foliage) grow to some 2ft(60cm) or more and arch over unless supported. Grow in pots of peat-based mix with about ⅓ added grit. Keep moist, letting the soil nearly dry out between each watering, and feed fortnightly during the summer. Repot spring. Increase by stem cuttings, 4-6in(10-15cm) long which are allowed to dry for some days before insertion, in summerr. *E. anguliger* (fishbone cactus) is grown mainly for its attractive flattened stems, which zigzag in almost alternate lobes on each side, the papery-white flowers are richly scented. A number of species and other genera have been used to produce some beautifully flowered hybrids including 'Carlvon Nicolai', pink; 'Cooperi', white, scented; 'Eastern Gold', yellow; 'London Beauty', red in spring, pink in autumn; 'London Glory', flame red with magenta glow; 'Padre', large pink; 'Reward', large yellow.

FAUCARIA (tiger jaws)
Fleshy-leaved succulents, the leaves curved inwards on top, toothed and spotted. They have yellow flowers. Grow in any free-draining potting mix. Keep well watered in autumn but much drier in winter and early spring, and grow in full light. Repot and increase by division when clumps are overcrowded or increase by cuttings in summer, inserted after the cut has dried. *F. tigrina* (tiger's jaw) forms rosette-like clumps of leaves which have long teeth, about 2in(5cm) tall. *F. tuberculosa*, dark green, white-tuberculed leaves with several stout teeth on the margin, about 3in(7.5cm) tall.

FEROCACTUS (barrel cactus)
Grown for their globular to cylindrical and sharply spiny bodies, these cacti rarely flower in cultivation. Grow in any free-draining mix and grow in full light, keep moist except in winter. Repot and increase by seed in spring. *F. latispinus* (devil's tongue) ribbed, globular to 1ft(30cm) or more, sharply spined, the central lower spine in each cluster longer and hooked. *F. wislizenii* (fishhook cactus) ribbed, globular when young but growing cylindrical to over 6ft(1.8m) sharply spined, several of the central spines in each cluster being hooked.

FREESIA
The many coloured, richly scented flowers of *F.* × *hybrida* make it a favourite indoor plant. The long leaves are narrow and about 1ft(30cm) tall, the flower stems longer, usually about 1½ft(45cm), and bear single or double flowers, in shades of mauve, purple, red, pink, orange, yellow, cream and white. Grow in any well-draining potting mix; potting several times from mid autumn to mid winter will give a succession of flower from winter into spring. Keep moist when growing and feed fortnightly when the flower spikes appear. Dry the plants gradually when the leaves yellow. Increase by offsets late summer or seed sown in spring.

GASTERIA (lawyer's- or ox-tongue)
Succulent foliage plants with thick leaves, usually arranged in two rows, with attractive markings. Reddish flowers are borne on arching 1ft(30cm) stems from spring to autumn. Grow in any free-draining potting mix kept moist except in winter when the plants should be much drier. Repot and increase by division or seed in spring. *G. brevifolia*, stemless, leaves in two ranks, broad, rounded tip, to 6in(15cm) long with transverse bands of white spots on dark green. *G. verrucosa*, stemless, leaves in two ranks, fine tapering and thick, to 6in(15cm) long and overlapping to make a plant about 6in(15cm) high.

163

GERBERA 12

Brilliant large daisy flowers in shades of pink, red, crimson, orange and yellow and in single or double forms characterize the modern strains of *G. jamesonii* (Barberton daisy). They are clump-forming perennials 8-24in(20-60cm) tall. Grow in pots of any good potting mix. Keep moist and feed fortnightly during the summer. The strain 'Happipot', which grows 8-12in(20-30cm) makes a good house plant flowering over a long period and requiring more water and feeding than most. Other strains generally are best in a conservatory except for bringing into the house to flower. Repot and increase by division or seed in spring.

GREVILLEA (spider flower)

Flowering shrubs and trees some of which are also grown for their attractive evergreen leaves. Grow in large tubs or pots of a lime-free mix. Repot spring and increase by seed then or by cuttings with a heel in summer. *G. juniperina* (*G. sulpherea*), small shrub, with narrow, sharp-pointed leaves, and plume-like clusters of yellow flowers, to 6ft(1.8m). *G. robusta* (silky oak) a tree in the wild and up to about 8ft(2.4m) in pots, grown as a foliage plant for its fern-like leaves. *G. rosmarinifolia*, small shrub, with narrow rosemary-like leaves, and short, dense spikes of rose-pink flowers, to 6ft(1.8m).

HAWORTHIA (wart plant)

Attractive foliage plants, the leaves usually in rosettes, and often marked with white. The small greenish-white flowers are insignificant. Grow in a free-draining mix, adding coarse sharp sand if necessary. Keep moist, ventilated and in full light. Repot and increase by division in spring. *H. attenuata*, leaves in rosettes up to 3in(7.5cm) long, tapering and spotted with white tubercules. *H. fasciata* (zebra haworthia), leaves in rosettes up to 1½in(4cm) long, tapering and spotted with white bands of tubercules. *H. truncata*, leaves in two ranks, incurved and fan shaped, the tops appearing sliced off and translucent, to ¾in(2cm) long.

HIBISCUS (rose mallow) 13

The large and lovely flowers of the shrub, *H. rosa-sinensis* (rose of China), may be borne on quite small plants. There are many hybrids available with flowers in shades of pink, apricot, orange, red and yellow besides the crimson of the species. All are well set off by the dark green glossy leaves, or in the case of 'Cooperi' its variegated leaves. Plants grow about 6-8ft(1.8-2.4m). Grow in pots of loam-based mix, shaded from strong sun. Repot in spring. Increase by cuttings in summer.

HIPPEASTRUM (Barbados lily)

Magnificently flowered bulbs, the flowers borne on a stout stem and set off by the broad strap-shaped arching leaves, make hippeastrum hybrids popular indoor plants. They are often sold under the name 'amaryllis'. The flowers are in shades of crimson, red, scarlet, pink and white, some varieties having streaks or other markings of a different colour. Most grow 15-24in(38-60cm) tall. Grow in pots of loam-based mix, only half burying the bulb. Keep moist while growing and feed fortnightly when in full growth. Dry the plants off if the foliage starts to yellow in late summer. Repot autumn and increase by offsets then.

JUSTICIA

This group has several attractive indoor plants of very different floral appearance. Only lightly shade them from sun in summer and grow them in loam- or peat-based mixes. Keep moist but drier after flowering until new shoots appear. Cut back after flowering. Repot in spring when cuttings may be taken and new plants raised annually. *J. brandegeana* (*Beloperone guttata* shrimp plant) drooping tails of pink and white flowers characterize this shrubby plant which may grow 3ft(90cm). *J. carnea* (*Jacobinia carnea* Brazilian plume), splendid dense heads of rose-pink flowers on a shrubby plant to 6ft(1.8m) tall. *J. rizzinii* (*Jacobinia pauciflora*), has flowers appearing singly from the leaf joints of brilliant yellow deepening to scarlet at their bases on a shrub to 2ft(60cm).

IMPATIENS (balsam, touch-me-not)

Easily grown, bushy plants often smothered in flowers, make these good indoor plants. Grow in pots of commercial mix, keep moist and feed occasionally when in flower. All may be raised from seed sown in spring, perennials also by cuttings through the year. *I. balsamina* (rose balsam), half-hardy annual with double or single flowers in shades of pink, red, blush and white, usually to 1½ft(45cm) or more but 8-10in(20-25cm) in the variety 'Tom Thumb'. *I. wallerana* (*I. holstii*, *I. sultanii* busy Lizzie, patient Lucy) tender perennial often grown as a half-hardy annual. A first class indoor flowering pot plant with flowers in a wide range of colours, single or double, some boldly marked with white in shades of crimson, red, scarlet, pink, orange, lilac and white; many strains producing plants from about 6-18in(15-45cm) usually.

IPOMOEA (morning glory)
Twining climbers with lovely but often short-lived flowers produced over a long period. Grow in pots of a commercial mix or in an indoor border. When flowers begin to show, feed fortnightly. Support as necessary. Sow seed after chipping or soaking in tepid water, in spring. *I. acuminata* (*I. learii* blue dawn flower) perennial to 20ft(6m), flowers purplish-blue turning carmine pink. *I. nil*, annual or perennial to 10ft(3m), flowers purplish shades, pink, blue or in the variety 'Scarlett O'Hara' crimson. *I. tricolor* (*I. rubrocaerulea*), perennial 6-10ft(1.8-3m), has a number of good varieties, 'Flying Saucers', flowers striped blue and white; 'Heavenly Blue', deep sky blue; 'Pearly Gates', white.

KALANCHOE (Palm beach bells)
A variable group of succulents, some grown for their brilliant flowers, some as foliage plants and others as curiosities their leaves bearing marginal plantlets. Grow in a well-draining mix adding extra sharp sand if necessary. Keep moist except in winter, then a bit drier. Repot spring and increase by seed then or by cuttings and plantlets in summer. *K. blossfeldiana*, glossy green leaves, bright yellow, red or orange flowers, 8-12in(20-30cm). *K. daigremontiana* (*Bryophyllum daigremontianum* devil's backbone), greyish-green leaves spotted brown with plantlets freely produced on their margins, 2-3ft(60-90cm). *K. tomentosa* (*K. pilosa* pussy ears, panda plant), silvery felted, rounded oblong leaves with brown margined tips, slowly reaching 10in(25cm) or more. *K. tubiflora* (*Bryophyllum tubiflorum* chandelier plant), remarkable cylindrical leaves, greyish spotted brown and bearing plantlets at the end, surmounted by a cluster of

hanging salmon to orange-red flowers, up to 3ft(90cm).

LAGERSTROEMIA
A beautifully flowered shrub, *L. indica* (crape myrtle) grows naturally to about 20ft(6m) but in cultivation much less if cut back annually or a dwarf strain is grown. The lovely flowers appear to have petals made of crepe paper, the petals stalked and coloured white, pink or crimson. It is deciduous with privet-like leaves. Grow in pot or tubs of loam-based mix or in an indoor border. Keep moist while growing and feed fortnightly in summer and autumn. Repot in spring and increase by seed then or cuttings in summer. Seed sown early of some strains will produce flowering plants in the same year. Established plants may be cut back to a half or less of the previous season's growth in spring.

LITHOPS (living stones, pebble plants)
Remarkable plants with two fused leaves, except at the top where a slit parts them and from where arises the large yellow to white daisy-like flower. Most of the body of the fused leaves is buried in nature and the plants spread sideways, forming clumps, rather than upwards. Grow in commercial mix to which a similar amount of coarse sharp sand has been added. Keep just moist from late spring to autumn and then dry. Repot every few years in spring and increase by seed then or by division in summer. *L. bella*, to 1in(2.5cm) wide and high, but forming clumps, leaves yellowish brown with darker greenish markings, white flowers. *L. lesliei*, to 1¾in(4.5cm) tall and nearly as wide, solitary or clump forming, purplish-green with green and rust markings, yellow flowers.

LOBIVIA (cob cactus)
Short cylindrical and globular-bodied small cacti with bright flowers. Grow in a loam-based mix mixed half and half with coarse sharp sand. Keep moist but allow to dry between each watering, and in a well ventilated, light position. Repot and increase by seed or offsets in spring. *L. famatimensis*, ribbed stems to 6in(15cm) tall, spines variable, flowers bright red to yellow or white. *L. heritrichiana*, ribbed globe to 4in(10cm) tall and wide, yellowish spines, and bright red flowers.

LUCULIA

An evergreen shrub with lovely pink to lilac-rose flowers, *L. gratissima* grows to about 6ft(1.8m). The flowers are scented, and come in large clusters from autumn to winter. Grow in pots or tubs of a loam-based mix or in an indoor border. Repot spring and increase by cuttings then. After flowering cut back stems by about ½-⅔.

LYCASTE

Orchids with oval pseudobulbs, deep green pleated leaves and attractive flowers. Grow in a mix of equal parts sphagnum moss, osmunda fibre, loam and leaf mould, in baskets or pots. Keep moist when leafy, almost dry when they have fallen. Feed occassionally during the summer and shade from strong sun but keep ventilated. Repot in spring and increase by division. *L. aromatica*, fragrant yellow flowers, leaves to 20in(50cm). *L. virginalis*, flowers variable, white, rose, pink, purple and crimson predominating or all white, leaves to 2ft(60cm) or more.

MAMMILLARIA (pincushion cactus)

Unribbed, spherical to cylindrical bodies bearing spirally arranged tubercules with long silvery spines and hairs, most branching from their base, and with flowers on top. Grow in a loam-based mix mixed half and half with coarse sharp sand, kept moist but allowed to dry between each watering, and in a light, well-ventilated position. Repot and increase by seed in spring or offsets in summer. *M. bocasana*, (powder puff or snowball cactus), stem cylindrical to 6in(15cm) tall, covered with white spines and hairs, the central spine from each areole yellowish, flowers creamy yellow. *M. prolifera* (silver cluster cactus), small cylindrical to 2½(6cm) tall, bristle like central yellowish spines surrounded by white woolly spines, clump forming, flowers yellowish.

MARANTA 14

A splendid foliage plant, *M. leuconeura* (prayer plant), has several attractively leaved varieties. *M. leuconeura erythroneura* has green leaves with darker green blotches between the red-coloured veins; *M.l. kerchoviana* (rabbit's foot) leaves light green with dark green to brown blotches; *M.l. leuconeura* (*M.l.* 'Massangeana'), dark green with silvery-grey veins. The young leaves tend to fold up in the evening. Plants spread horizontally and so remain fairly prostrate. Grow in pots of commercial mix, keep moist and feed in the summer when they should be shaded. Repot and increase by division in spring.

MILTONIA (pansy orchid)

Large, rather flat-faced flowers are carried on arching stems from pseudobulbs with two leaves. Grow in a mix of two parts osmunda fibre to one of sphagnum moss. Keep moist; shade and syringe in hot weather. Increase by division in spring or autumn. There are many splendidly flowered hybrids available with flowers in blends and mixes of white, rose, yellow, purple, crimson, red, cream and violet, on stems 8-24in(20-60cm) long.

MONSTERA

One of the largest growing popular house plants, *M. deliciosa* (Swiss cheese plant), will do even better in a warm conservatory or garden room. The dark green leaves develop large perforations and grow rapidly in sufficient warmth and light. They may be kept low at 7-10ft(2-3m) but will grow up to 20-25ft(6-7.5m) otherwise. Grow in peat-based mix kept moist and feed regularly spring to autumn. Provide support, preferably a moss-covered stake into which the aerial roots may twine and which should be kept moist by syringing. Repot spring to summer. Increase by stem tip cuttings with one leaf in summer.

NEPHROLEPIS (sword fern) 15

Very decorative ferns seen to advantage from hanging baskets, *N. exaltata*, a fern with fronds to 3ft(90cm) or more, has many varieties. They include 'Bostoniensis', Boston fern, with drooping fronds; 'Elegantissima' with compact fronds; and 'Rooseveltii' with dark green fringed leaflets. Grow in a commercial mix preferably with some added sphagnum moss kept moist but not overwet, and feed fortnightly in summer. Repot and increase by division in spring.

NERINE

Lovely autumn flowering bulbs with narrow, arching leaves and growing 1-2ft(30-60cm) tall. Grow in pots of a loam-based mix, burying the bulb but not its neck. Water when growth appears, letting the pots almost dry out before watering again and keep watering similarly until the leaves yellow and the pot is allowed to dry out. Feed fortnightly when in full growth. Repot and increase by offsets in spring. *N. bowdenii*, almost hardy and a fine pot plant, flowers in clusters with long wavy pink petals. *N. sarniensis* (Guernsey lily) more compact clusters of crimson to pink flowers; a number of splendid varieties have been developed such as 'Miss E. Cator' with deep red flowers, and 'Nicholas' with white and red striped flowers.

NERIUM (oleander)
Floriferous and evergreen, *N. oleander* (oleander or rose bay), is a shrub to 6ft(1.8m) or more with tough, willowy leaves. The flowers, double or single, are in shades of deep red, pink and creamy white or white; the variety 'Variegata' has creamy-margined leaves and pink flowers. Grow in loam-based mix and keep well watered but less so in winter, feeding fortnightly in summer. Flowering may be restricted in pots too small. Repot in spring and increase by seed then or cuttings in summer.

NOTOCACTUS (ball cactus)
Small cacti with globular to shortly cylindrical bodies, and bright flowers. Grow in a half and half mixture of a loam-based mix and coarse sharp sand. Keep moist but allow to dry between each watering and in a sunny, ventilated position. Repot and increase by seed or offsets in spring. *N. haselbergii* (scarlet ball cactus) globular to 5in(12.5cm) tall, ribbed with yellowish spines, and topped by brilliant orange to red flowers. *N. ottonis*, to 4in(10cm) ribbed with yellowish to brown spines, flowers bright yellow.

ODONTOGLOSSUM
Beautiful orchids with long arching sprays of flowers, many species and hybrids are available in a wide range of flower colour and form. Grow in pots or baskets of a two to one mix of osmunda fibre and sphagnum moss to which a little coarse sharp sand has been added. Keep well ventilated but in a humid atmosphere and shaded from summer sun. Repot and increase by division in spring or autumn. *O. crispum* (lace orchid), a very beautifully flowered

plant, up to twelve flowers on arching stems 18-24in(45-60cm) long, white to blush pink frilled petals with a yellow centre marked with red, or in the variety 'Lyoth Arctic' pure white, while 'Purpurascens' is heavily tinted pink, two leaves to 15in(38cm). *O. grande* (tiger orchid), has large flowers, on 1ft(30cm) stems, brown-banded yellow petals, a creamy-red marked centre, though the many hybrids and varieties have flowers in a wide range of colours in various combinations of white, pink, rose, red, crimson, yellow and cream, two leaves to 14in(35cm) in length.

OPUNTIA (prickly pear)
Mainly shrubby, branching cacti with flat round to pear shaped stems or pads spotted with groups of spines. The flowers are usually red or yellow. Grow in pots of ⅔ proprietary mix and ⅓ coarse sharp sand. Keep watered except in winter when the soil should be only just moist. Repot spring and increase by seed then or detached pads in summer. *O. decumbens*, semi-prostrate to 1½ft(45cm), flowers yellow turning reddish. *O. ficus-indica* (Indian fig), tall eventually to about 18ft(5.5m), flowers yellow, fruit purple, red, yellow or white and edible. *O. microdasys* (bunny ears), pads thickly spotted with yellowish spine groups, or in the variety 'Albispina', polka dot cactus, white spotted, to 3ft(90cm) flowers yellow.

PASSIFLORA (Passion flower)
Beautifully flowered climbers, many developing excellent edible fruit. Grow in pots or tubs of loam-based mix and provide substantial support for the plants to climb on, at the same time, or grow in an indoor border. Repot if necessary in spring when crowded plants may be thinned. Increase by seed, which may need soaking, spring or by cuttings in summer. *P. caerulea* (blue passion flower) up to 30ft(9m), petals white to blush, filamentary corona banded blue, white and purple, fruit yellow not of culinary interest, nearly fully hardy. *P. edulis* (purple granadilla passion fruit), to 25ft(7.5m) or more, petals white, filamentary corona banded purple and white, fruit greenish-yellow to greenish-purple, edible. *P. mollissima* (banana passion fruit), to 30ft(9m) or more, petals blush and pink, fruit rounded oblong to 2½in(6.4cm), yellow, edible.

PELLAEA (cliff brake)

An attractive fern with almost round leaflets which lengthen with age, *P. rotundifolia* (button fern) is an excellent room plant. The fronds arch over and grow to about 1ft(30cm) long. Grow in pots of peat-based mix in a shady position. Feed established plants from spring to autumn. Repot and increase by division in spring, repotting only needed every few years.

PELARGONIUM (storksbill, geranium)

Popular pot plants grown for flower and foliage and of bushy or trailing form. Grow in loam-based mix kept moist during the growing season but drier in winter. Feed fortnightly in summer. Repot spring. Increase by seed sown early in the year, by cuttings in summer. *P. capitatum* (rose scented geranium), to 2ft(60cm), leaves felty, small, roundish, shallowly lobed and scented, flowers small, pink. *P. crispum* (lemon geranium), to 3ft(90cm) leaves fan shaped and crisply curled, scented and in the variety 'Variegatum' with cream markings, flowers small pink. *P.* × *domesticum* (regal pelargonium), showy geranium, shrubby to 15-24in(38-60cm), leaves large, shallowly lobed, large flowers in large clusters in shades of crimson, purple, red, pink and white usually with a darker blotch, sometimes picotee or bicoloured according to variety, such as 'Aztec' red veined darker and white picote edged, 'Grandma Fischer' salmon blotched black. *P.* × *hortorum* (zonal geranium), 6in-6ft(15cm-1.8m), leaves usually large, often with a strong horseshoe zone of shades of brown, sometimes marked with other colours, shallow lobed to zigzag, large heads of brilliant flowers from white to pink, red, orange, scarlet and crimson, according to variety, such as 'Irene Flame' orange pink, 'Picasso' fluorescent cerise red; 'Bronze Queen' light green leaves with brown zone, red flowers. *P. peltatum* (ivy leaved geranium), slender trailing or climbing stems 3ft(90cm) or more, leaves fleshy, ivy shaped, flowers white, pink, lilac, carmine according to variety, such as 'Galilee' bright pink, double, 'L'Elegante' leaves splashed white and rose tinted, flowers white, lilac tinged.

PHILODENDRON

Large-leaved climbing foliage plants, the leaves often attractively coloured. Grow in large pots, or indoor borders, of peat-based mix. Keep moist and warm, humid and shaded in summer, and provide suitable support, such as moss covered stakes for climbers. Repot spring. Increase by cuttings in summer. *P. domesticum* (*P. hastatum* spade leaf, elephant's ear), large leaves up to 2ft(60cm) long and half as wide, often less in pots, climbing up to 5ft(1.5m) in pots. *P. melanochrysum* (*P. andreanum* black-gold or velour philodendron), large leaves to 2½ft(75cm) long, 1ft(30cm) wide or less in pots, dark blackish-green leaves with a velvet sheen, climbing up to 6ft(1.8m) in pots. *P. scandens* (heart leaf), has a popular variety, *P. scandens oxycardium* (*P. cordatum*, *P. oxycardium* parlour ivy), with glossy green leaves to 1ft(30cm) long, 9in(23cm) wide, climbing to 10ft(3m) in pots.

PILEA 16

Small evergreen plants with attractive foliage. Grow in pots of a peat-based mix. Keep humid and shade from sun in summer. Repot in spring and increase by cuttings then or in summer. *P. cadierei* (aluminium plant), bushy to 1ft(30cm), leaves boldly marked with silvery patches between the veins. *P. microphylla* (*P. muscosa* artillery plant), short-lived shrubby plant to 1ft(30cm) leaves small, mossy green, flowers insignificant but discharge puffs of pollen. *P. repens* (black leaf panamiga), dwarf, spreading, leaves bronze above, purple below, quilted.

PLATYCERIUM (staghorn fern)

A magnificent fern, *P. bifurcatum* (*P. alcicorne*), has leaves of two types, rounded ones that surround its support, and fertile ones that grow up and divide into long lobes that may arch over; 1½-2½ft(45-76cm). Grow in hanging baskets or attached to bark, in a half-and-half mix of sphagnum moss and a peat-based mix. On bark, wrap the roots in a ball of the mix and fix with wire. Water spring to autumn but keep drier in winter. Repot spring and increase by detaching plantlets then.

PLECTRANTHUS

Attractive evergreen plants and easy to grow. Grow in pots of a commercial mix shaded from strong sun. Repot in spring and increase then by division or cuttings. *P. coleoides* (candle plant) leaves green or edged with white in the variety 'Marginatus', to

13 *Hibiscus rosa-sinensis* var (rose of China)
15 *Nephrolepis exaltata* 'Elegantissima' (sword fern)
17 *Plumbago auriculata* (Cape leadwort)

14 *Maranta leuconeura kerchoviana* (rabbit's foot)
16 *Pilea cadierei* (aluminium plant)
18 *Primula malacoides* (fairy or baby primrose)

3ft(90cm) but usually less in pots, flowers white and purple in an 8in(20cm) spike. *P. oertendahlii* (prostrate coleus, Swedish ivy), creeping, bronzy-green leaves, silver veined above and purple below, about 15in(38cm) flowers lilac pink in a 1ft(30cm) spike.

PLUMBAGO (leadwort) 17
A lovely semi-climbing plant when covered with its light blue flowers, *P. auriculata* (*P. capensis* Cape leadwort), needs tying in to some support. Evergreen, oblong leaves to 2in(5cm) on a plant to 10ft(3m). Keep in bounds by pruning every spring. Grow in pots of loam-based mix and feed fortnightly in summer, keep drier in winter. Increase by cuttings in summer.

PRIMULA (primrose) 18
Several primula species have been developed to make excellent pot plants with long flowering periods, and although they are perennials they are usually grown as annuals. Grow in pots of commercial mix and keep moist. Sow seed in spring and summer. *P. malacoides* (fairy or baby primrose), up to 1½ft(45cm) depending on variety, leaves oval to elliptic, flowers in several clusters circling the flower stem, single or double, in shades of pink, red, lilac, carmine and white. *P. obconica* (German primrose) upto 1ft(30cm) depending on variety, leaves rather rounded to elliptic and covered with hairs which may irritate some people, flowers in large heads, single, in shades of pink, red, lilac, blue, purple, crimson and white. *P. sinensis* (Chinese primrose) up to 1ft(30cm) depending on variety, rather stiff upright leaves, lobed and toothed, flowers in large heads, single, in bright colours including shades of pink, red, orange, blue, purple and white.

PTERIS (brake)
Beautiful clump-forming evergreen ferns with delicate fronds. Grow in pots of peat-based mix. Repot in spring and increase by division then. *P. cretica* (Cretan brake, ribbon fern) up to 1½ft(45cm), fronds deeply divided, light green or white centred in 'Albo-lineata'. *P. ensiformis* (sword brake), up to 20in(50cm), fronds deeply divided, deep green or silvery centred in 'Victoriae' (Victoria brake, silver table fern). *P. tremula* (Australian brake, trembling bracken) fronds 1-2ft(30-60cm) in pots, twice this, or more in an indoor border, heavily divided, graceful, bright green.

RHOEO
A first class small foliage plant, *R. spathacea* (*R. discolor*), is burdened with many popular names including boat lily, purple-leaved spiderwort and Moses-on-a-raft. The popular names refer to fancied resemblances seen in the shape of the white flowers which nestle in the crowded leaf rosettes. The fleshy leaves are shining green above and purple below and up to 1ft(30cm) long or with yellowish stripes in 'Variegata'. Grow in a commercial mix. Repot spring and increase by seed then or cuttings in summer.

REBUTIA (crown cactus)
Small, free-flowering, globular cacti whose flowers develop in a circle around the plants which are covered with spiny tubercules spirally arranged. The plants form clumps. Grow in a loam-based mix and an equal amount of coarse sharp sand. Keep moist but let dry out between each watering and grow in a sunny, well ventilated position. Repot and increase by offsets spring. *R. deminuta*, about 2½in(6.5cm) tall, orange-red flowers. *R. minuscula*, red-crown, up to 1½in(4cm) tall and slightly broader, crimson-red flowers. *R. pseudodeminuta* (wallflower-crown) up to 2½in(6.5cm) tall, flowers yellow.

RHOICISSUS (African grape)
A very popular foliage plant, *R. rhomboidea*, (the grape ivy) is similar to *Cissus rhombifolia* (Venezuelan treebine), and one may sometimes be sold for the other. The dark green leaves are composed of three rhomboidal leaflets and smother the climbing stems which may reach to 20ft(6m) but are easily kept down by pruning. Grow in pots of a loam-based mix and provide support for the tendrils to cling to. Keep lightly shaded and ventilated in summer. Repot annually in spring and increase by cuttings in late spring or summer.

SAINTPAULIA (African violet)
A popular though sometimes suffering house plant, *S. ionantha* (African violet), has rosettes of leaves which set off the attractive flowers. The leaves are

fleshy, usually dark green though there are several variegated varieties too, and the flowers are in many shades of violet, blue, carmine and pink as well as white, some flowers may have the petals edged or marked with another colour, according to variety. The plants are usually about 4-5in(10-12.5cm) tall and form clumps. Grow in pots of peat-based mix kept moist but not soaking and feed fortnightly except through winter. Allow the compost to nearly dry out between waterings. Keep warm and draught free, a 60°F(16°C) minimum is preferable but plants will grow below this. Repot early summer and increase by division then or leaf cuttings through summer.

SALPIGLOSSIS
A large flowered half hardy annual, *S. sinuata* (painted tongue, velvet trumpet flower), is sometimes offered under a variety of other names including *grandiflora* and *superbissima*. Several strains are available and grow 1½-3ft(45-90cm) tall, the slender stems bearing light green leaves and surmounted by several beautiful flowers. The flowers are in shades of violet, crimson, red, pink, orange, and yellow which is often veined with a darker colour. Grow in pots of loam-based mix and keep warm. Sow seed in spring for summer and autumn flowering; sow in late summer to autumn for winter and spring flowering if a minimum of about 60°F(16°C) is possible.

SEDUM (stonecrop)
Succulent plants with attractive leaves and flowers, most sedums are easy to grow in pots of a well-draining mix; add extra sharp sand if necessary to a loam-based mix. Keep drier in winter, otherwise moist but allowing the pots to nearly dry out between waterings, and in a light, ventilated spot. Repot spring to autumn. Increase by seed in spring, cuttings in summer. *S. bellum*, blue-green spoon-shaped leaves are borne on mealy stems 3-6in(7.5-15cm) long, and white flowers late spring to early summer. *S. brevifolium*, prostrate, creeping stems forming clumps about 1ft(30cm) across, leaves egg-shaped globular, grey-green sometimes flushed pink, covered with meal, flowers white summer. *S. sieboldii* (October plant), stems arching, 6-9in(15-23cm) long, leaves flattish, blue-green or marked with cream in 'Medio-variegatum', flowers pink, autumn.

SENECIO (cineraria)
Popular pot plants with large heads of flowers in a wide range of bright colours, *S. × hybridus* (cineraria), grows 1-2½ft(30-75cm) according to variety. The large, roundish leaves set off, unless obscured by, the flowers which are violet, purple, crimson, red, pink shades and white, sometimes with a white eye. Grow in pots of loam-based mix, keep moist and feed when flowering every 10 days. Keep ventilated and shaded from strong sun. Sow seed annually in spring for winter flowers, in summer for spring to summer flowers.

SETCREASEA
A superb purple-leaved foliage plant, *S. pallida* 'Purple Heart' (*S. purpurea*), is a sprawling plant up to 15in(38cm). The leaves are 4-6in(10-15cm) long the edges turned up. Flowers are pinkish purple on purple stems. Grow in proprietary potting mix. Repot spring and increase by division then or cuttings spring to autumn.

SELAGINELLA (spike moss)
Evergreen foliage plants with a rather mossy to ferny appearance and easy to grow. Grow in a moist, peat-based mix. Keep humid, draught free and shaded from sun. Repot and increase by division in spring. *S. apoda* (meadow spike moss), prostrate, spreading, stems to 4in(10cm) long, densely leaved, mossy. *S. lepidophylla* (resurrection plant, rose of Jericho), frond-like stems to 4in(10cm) long, tufted, leafy. When dry, curls into a ball and expands again with moisture.

SOLANUM
The plants described here, whether bushy or climbing, all have rather potato-like flowers, white to lavender blue, borne singly or in clusters. The bushy plants are grown for their brightly coloured fruits, the climbers for their flowers. Grow in pots of loam-based mix or an indoor border and feed established plants fortnightly during the growing season. Raise the bushy fruiting plants annually by seed, the climbers may be increased by cuttings in summer. Prune the climbers back each spring. *S. capsicastrum* (false Jerusalem or winter cherry), bushy shrub, 1-2ft(30-60cm), fruit scarlet, orange, white according

to variety. *S. jasminoides* (potato vine), shrubby climber, 8-15ft(2.4-4.5m), flowers in large clusters, white tinged lavender, or white in 'Album'. *S. pseudocapsicum* (Jerusalem or Christmas cherry) bushy shrub, 1-4ft(30-120cm) fruit scarlet, orange to yellow according to variety. *S. wendlandii* (giant potato creeper, paradise flower), strong-growing shrubby climber, 15ft(4.5m) or more, prickly, flowers in large clusters, lavender blue.

SOLEIROLIA (Helxine)

A mat-forming creeping plant, no more than about 1-3in(2-7cm) tall, which will cascade down pot sides, *S. soleirolii* (*H. soleirolii*), has a large number of popular names including baby's tears, Irish moss and Corsican curse. Useful as ground cover beneath other pot or border plants but can become a weed, the small leaves on wiry stems are densely packed. Grow in loam-based mix and shade from strong sun. Increase by detaching pieces in summer.

SPREKELIA

Grown for its beautiful, rich crimson flowers, *S. formosissima* (Jacobean or Aztec lily) is a choice bulbous plant. Strap-shaped leaves, to 1ft(30cm) long appear after the flowers which top their 1ft(30cm) stems. The flowers are about 4in(10cm) across and have an orchid-like appearance. Grow in pots of loam-based mix, leaving the bulb neck above soil level. Keep moist while growing and feed fortnightly when in full growth. Dry the plants off when the leaves start to yellow. Repot autumn and increase by offsets then.

STRELITZIA (bird of paradise)

A striking plant when in flower, *S. reginae* (bird of paradise flower) is an evergreen perennial. Leaf blades to 1½ft(45cm) on long stalks, the plant clump 3-4ft(90-120cm) tall. The orange and blue flowers are carried horizontally, to 8in(20cm) long, and appear to burst out of the end of the stem. Grow in loam-based mix in pots or in indoor borders. Water freely in summer, less in winter. Repot autumn or spring. Increase by division or seed in spring.

TECOPHILAEA

The strong gentian-blue flowers of *T. cyanocrocus* (Chilean crocus), make it an outstanding pot plant. The two or three green leaves are up to 5in(12.5cm) long, the flower stems up to 4in(10cm) and carry their beautiful rather spreading petalled crocus-like flowers in spring. Grow in pots of loam-based mix kept almost dry until growth commences and then watered until the leaves begin to yellow when the pots should be kept almost dry again. Repot in autumn and increase by offsets then or by seed in spring.

THUNBERGIA

The beautifully flowered twining climbers described here are all perennials but black-eyed Susan is often raised as an annual. Grow in indoor borders or pots of loam-based mix kept drier over winter, and feed pot-grown plants regularly in summer. Keep warm and preferably in a slightly humid atmosphere. Shade against strong sun. Repot and increase by seed in spring or by cuttings in summer. *T. alata* (black-eyed Susan) leafy climber to 10ft(3m), flowers white, cream or orange with a dark centre. *T. grandiflora* (blue trumpet or clock vine), woody climber to 20ft(6m) flowers in hanging clusters, blue. *T. gregorii* (*T. gibsonii*), similar to black-eyed Susan but the flowers are orange.

TRADESCANTIA (spiderwort)

Popular pot-grown plants mainly grown for the forms with variegated foliage, and most of which are suitable for hanging baskets. Grow in pots or baskets of any good potting mix. Keep watered well in summer and shaded from strong sun. Plants are apt to get straggly and worn out and, while they may be repotted in spring, it is usually better to start with new plants from cuttings taken in spring for they root easily. Established plants appreciate fortnightly feeding in summer. *T. albiflora* (wandering Jew, inch plant) trailing stems to 2ft(60cm) or more, leaves plain green or in the larger leaved variety 'Albovittáta' (giant white inch plant), white striped. *T. blossfeldiana* (flowering inch plant), trailing to semi-erect purple stems to 9in(23cm) long, leaves green above, purple, hairy below, or cream-striped leaves in 'Variegata', flowers white-eyed purple in small clusters. *T. fluminensis* (wandering Jew, speedy Jenny), similar to *T. albiflora*, but leaves flushed purple below and in 'Variegata' leaves are striped white to cream.

VALLOTA

The lovely scarlet flowers of *V. speciosa* (*V. purpurea* Scarborough lily) are borne on stems to 2ft(60cm) tall. The strap-like leaves are present through the year and may also grow to 2ft(60cm) long. Grow in pots of good potting mix kept watered and fed fortnightly in summer, and just moist through winter. Repot only every few years and increase by offsets then.

ZANTEDESCHIA (*Richardia* calla)

The striking spathes make zantedeschias attractive pot plants. Grow in pots of a good potting mix kept just moist until growth starts and then water freely until flowering finishes, feeding every 10 days while in flower. Gradually dry off as the leaves yellow. Repot late winter to early spring and increase by offsets or division then or by seed in spring. *Z. aethiopica* (*Z. africana* florist's calla, arum lily) dark green leaves on stems to 3ft(90cm), white-spathed flowers on stems to 4ft(1.2m) or more. *Z. albomaculata* (*Z. melanoleuca* spotted or black-throated calla), green leaves with semi-transparent white spots on stems to 3ft(90cm), cream-spathed flowers with a purple blotch inside, on a slender stem. *Z. elliottiana* (golden calla) dark green leaves with transparent white spots on stems to 2ft(60cm) yellow-spathed flowers with a green base on stems to 2ft(60cm) *Z. rehmannii* (pink calla), bright green leaves sometimes spotted or streaked transparent white on stems to 2ft(60cm), pale to deep pink to purplish spathes.

ZEBRINA

An attractive-leaved plant, *Z. pendula* (wandering Jew inch plant), is similar in appearance and habit to *Tradescantia*, and suitable for pots or hanging baskets. The typical form has green leaves striped with silver above, purple below, the variety 'Purpusii' (*Z. purpusii*) has leaves purple-green above and bright purple below, while 'Quadricolor' has leaves strikingly striped with metallic green, green, pink and white above, purple below. Grow these plants in any good potting mix, keep well watered and shaded from strong sun in summer. Repot and increase by cuttings in spring.

List 3 Plants for unheated conservatories, extensions and living rooms

These are suitable for places in which the temperature may occasionally fall to freezing point, but where some form of heat is used during prolonged cold spells.

AGAPANTHUS (African lily)   19

Superb clump-forming herbaceous plants for large pots or tubs, with large heads of flowers in shades of blue or white, and long strap-shaped leaves which are evergreen or deciduous. Grow in loam-based mix and feed when growing. Repot every few years in spring and increase by division then or by seed. *A. africanus* (*A. umbellatus* blue African lily), evergreen, to 2ft(60cm) flowers violet blue. *A. campanulatus*, deciduous, to 2½ft(75cm), flowers blue. *A. praecox* (*A. umbellatus*), evergreen, 2-4ft(60-120cm) according to variety of which there are a number, flowers from deep to light blue and white. There are also a number of good hybrids from various species with flowers of dark to light blue and white, of varying height.

ALOYSIA (*Lippia*)

The fragrant foliage has long made *A. triphylla* (*L. citriodora* lemon verbena) a favourite plant. It is a shrub, 5-10ft(1.5-3m) or more tall, with willow-like leaves and many small spikes of whitish-lavender flowers. Grow in large pots of loam-based mix kept well watered and ventilated in summer when the pots may also be put outside. Repot every two years in spring and increase by cuttings or seed then.

ARUM

Growing from corms, arums have attractive flower spathes and leaves. Grow in pots of loam-based potting mix kept just moist until growth starts and then water freely until flowering finishes, feeding every fortnight while in flower. Dry off as the leaves yellow. Repot in autumn and increase by offsets then or when the plant is dormant and by seed when ripe. *A. creticum* to 1½ft(45cm) spathes white to yellow. *A. palaestinum* (Solomon's lily, black calla) to 20in(50cm) spathes greenish on the outside but blackish-purple inside.

CAMELLIA
Beautiful flowering evergreens, most camellias will make attractive pot plants and in particular the many varieties of *C. japonica* (common camellia). These have flowers 3-5in(7.5-12.5cm) across, double or single and in shades of crimson, deep orange-red and pink to white, and some bicolours. Grow in large pots of lime-free potting mix, keep moist but not soaking, and feed while in growth. After flowering bury the pots outdoors in spring and bring in again in late autumn or keep in a cool place indoors. Repot in spring or autumn and increase by cuttings in autumn. Camellias should only be repotted when they have outgrown their container. Prune lightly in late spring or early summer to keep plants within bounds – the common camellia could grow to 20ft(6m) or more.

CAMPANULA (bellflower)
The two bellflowers described here are very different in character, one an excellent trailing plant for hanging baskets, the other a striking tall plant. Grow in a loam-based mix in an airy situation. Repot and increase *C. isophylla* by division or cuttings in spring; increase *C. pyramidalis* by offset rosettes or seed in spring. *C. isophylla* (Italian bellflower), trailing stems to 1ft(30cm) or more covered with open, star-shaped blue or white flowers in late summer; keep only just moist in winter. *C. pyramidalis* (chimney bellflower) to 5ft(1.5m) a tall pyramid of blue or white bell-shaped flowers in summer; treat as a biennial.

CAMPSIS (trumpet creeper)
Luxuriantly foliaged climbing plants for an indoor border, with brilliant orange to red flowers. Grow in well drained but moisture-retentive soil. Increase by detaching suckers or by seed in spring, by cuttings in late summer. Keep in bounds by pruning back in spring. *C. grandiflora* (Chinese trumpet creeper) to

30ft(9m) or more, scarlet red flowers in late summer. *C. radicans* (trumpet creeper) to 40ft(12m) or more, orange shading to scarlet flowers in late summer. *C. × tagliabuana*, a hybrid between the two species above and intermediate between the two but has a fine variety, 'Mme Galen' with deep salmon flowers.

CAPPARIS (caper)
The culinary caper is provided by the flower buds, but the flowers are brilliant white with long violet mauve stamens from spring to summer. A shrubby plant, usually spiny, to about 4ft(1.2m). Grow in pots of well-drained mix adding extra coarse sand as necessary, and place in a sunny position but ventilate in hot weather. Repot in spring and increase by heeled cuttings in summer.

CAPSICUM (pepper)
The ornamental peppers are different varieties of the red or green peppers, or chilli, grown for the kitchen. They are varieties of *C. annuum* and have red, orange or yellow fruit in various shapes from round to long and pointed, according to variety, and reach about 1½ft(45cm) in height. Plants are usually raised annually. Grow in pots of loam-based mix. Increase by seed in spring.

CHRYSANTHEMUM   20
Florist's chrysanthemums are available in many forms – from the tall, 4-5ft(1.2-1.5m), Incurved and Reflexed petalled types to the charming Charm, 3ft(1m) high, and Cascade, 3-5ft(1-1.5m) long, forms. Other types are Intermediate, half way between the first two; Single, with large daisy-shaped flowers; Anemone centred, single but the centre cushioned with long florets; Pompon, small rounded to globular flowers on 1ft(30cm) stems; Miscellaneous, includes all those that do not fall into the other catagories, such as the Charm and Cascade forms, as well as Spider, Spoon and Spray. Grow in pots of loam-based mix in a sunny sheltered spot until late autumn. Then bring them indoors and keep watered and well ventilated. After flowering keep them almost dry, cutting the plants down to 6in(15cm) and keep in a frost free place until spring when new shoots from the base may be used to raise plants for the following season. Many of the Miscellaneous

group may also be raised annually from seed. Cuttings from bought pot plants may not be the same as the originals due to chemicals used by commercial nurseries to determine growth. The choice of varieties, of all sizes and colours, is enormous.

COBAEA

A fast growing climber, *C. scandens* (cup and saucer vine), is a long-flowering perennial indoors though also grown as an annual outside. The typical plant has flowers which start green, turn cream and then purplish violet, while in 'Alba' the flowers remain creamy white. In favourable conditions the plant may reach 30ft(9m) or more. Grow in an indoor border or in pots of weakly fertilized mix. Pinching back will help to bush the plant out and should be done regularly. Repot if required in spring and increase by seed then.

CRINUM (spider lily)

Large bulbous plants needing plenty of room, crinums have beautiful lily-shaped flowers in large clusters. Grow in large pots of loam-based mix planting the bulbs with the top ⅓ above soil. Keep moist while growing, and feed fortnightly then, shade from strong sun. Repot every 2-3 years and increase by offsets then or by seed which may take some years to germinate. *C. bulbispermum*, leaves to 3ft(90cm) long, flowers in heads of up to 12 on a 1ft(30cm) stem, white flushed red outside. *C. moorei*, similar but larger than *C. bulbispermum*, flowers on stems to 2ft(60cm), rose. *C. × powellii*, a hybrid between the two species above, similar in size to *C. moorei*, flowers reddish to purplish or white in variety 'Alba'.

CYCLAMEN

The florist's cyclamen, derived from *C. persicum*, is one of the most charming of pot plants and available in a wide range of flower colour from crimson through deep magenta, red, pink to white and sometimes bicoloured. Varieties with beautifully marked leaves have been developed. They are not too difficult to grow, the most likely killer being kindness: too much heat or watering to excess. Grow in pots of peat-based mix, keep just moist, water more freely when in growth but dry off in a cool, dry place

when the leaves start to yellow in spring. Repot in late summer into fresh moist compost, keep just moist until growth starts again, the corm should be planted with the top at or just above soil level. The situation should be light but not in sun, cool 45-60°F(7-16°C), the lower temperature at night. Increase by seed in autumn or spring.

FATSIA

A splendid, bold foliage plant, *F. japonica* (*Aralia japonica* Japanese fatsia), has rich glossy green, hand-shaped leaves with 5-11 lobes, up to 16in(40cm) across. Balls of small, whitish flowers are borne on a branched spike. The plant might grow 16-20ft(5-6m) but usually much less in pots. The variety 'Moseri' is larger leaved, compact but vigorous while 'Variegata' has cream-margined leaves. Grow in pots or tubs of any good mix. Repot spring and increase by removing suckers or seed then.

FUCHSIA 21

There are hundreds of varieties of this popular flowering shrub, raised from a number of species, and in a wide range of colours. The flowers have two distinct rows of petals, each usually of a different colour or shade in crimson, purple, violet, red, orange, pink or white. Shape of bush varies from upright and dwarf to tall growing, and some are pendent, depending on variety. Grown as bushes they will be about 2ft(60cm) high, but treated as standards, many will reach 3-5ft(1-1.5m). The leaves are usually green but some varieties have golden or variegated leaves. Grow in loam-based mix in pots, tubs or hanging baskets and feed fortnightly in summer. Repot annually in spring and increase by seed or cuttings then, or cuttings in summer. Rooted cuttings will need pinching out to increase bushiness or the number of hanging branches. Established plants should be cut back annually, cutting the previous season's growth down to a few inches/centimetres when repotting.

HEDERA (ivy)

Easy-to-grow foliage plants, ivies have leaves of various shapes, sizes and colour ranging from deep to light green or yellow, and may be variegated in various ways. Climbing or creeping plants, easy to

19 *Agapanthus africanus* (blue African lily)
21 *Fuchsia* var
23 *Punica granatum* 'Nana' (dwarf pomegranate)

20 *Chrysanthemum* Pompon type
22 *Narcissus* var
24 *Sarracenia purpurea* (common pitcher plant)

control by pruning. Grow in pots or hanging baskets of any good mix, and preferably shade from strong sun. Repot spring or autumn and increase by cuttings from spring to autumn. *H. canariensis* (Canary Island ivy) large leaves, about 6in/15cm, shallowly lobed, glossy dark green or in 'Variegata' ('Gloire de Marengo'), greyish green with cream margins. *H. helix* (English or common ivy), extremely variable, usually 5 lobed leaves, 3in(7.5cm), dark green. Varieties include 'Buttercup', yellow leaves; 'Conglomerata', small, wavy, green leaves, congested on stiff, slow growing stems; 'Cristata', light to medium green leaves, very wavy; 'Glacier', small, triangular, grey and green leaves, flushed pink with white margins; 'Gold Heart', small, dark green leaves with yellow centres; 'Sagittifolia', long arrow-shaped leaves, grey green; 'Sagittifolia Variegata', long arrow-shaped leaves, grey-green blotched and marked white.

HYACINTHUS (hyacinth)

Well known as forced bulbs for Christmas flowering the popular varieties of *H. orientalis* have heavy spikes of flowers in shades of purple, red, pink, yellow, blue and white, and are often very fragrant, most about 8-10in(20-25cm) tall. More graceful, and easier to force, is *H. orientalis albulus* (Roman hyacinth) with white to blue flowers. For winter flower, pot the bulbs from late summer to early autumn in any commercial mix, in pots or bowls with drainage holes or in bulb fibre for containers without holes, and leaving the nose of the bulbs just above the surface. Place the potted bulbs in a cool place outdoors where they may be buried, covered with a layer of soil, peat or weathered ashes. When they are well rooted and the shoots are 2-3in(5-7.5cm) tall – after some weeks – bring the pots into a cool, well-ventilated place and keep them moist. Specially prepared bulbs are also available for early flowering, or grow Roman hyacinths. It is important not to provide too high a temperature, about 60°F(16°C), or poor flowers and plants will develop.

HYDRANGEA

The huge heads of flowers, in shades of blue, red, pink and white, and ease of cultivation, have made the forms of *H. macrophylla* very popular pot plants.

Those with large balls of flowers are derived from *H. macrophylla macrophylla*, those with flat heads known as lace caps from *H. macrophylla normalis*. To 5ft(1.5m) or more. There are a large number of excellent named varieties and choice must depend on the colour and type required. Grow in pots of commercial mix and keep moist, and shade from strong sun. Feed fortnightly when in flower. Cut back after flowering. Repot annually. Increase by cuttings from spring to autumn, the earlier cuttings resulting in larger, branched plants the next year. Many of the pink to red varieties turn blue in acid soil mixes or with the aid of bluing agents.

JASMINUM (jasmine)

The two lovely shrubs described here can provide masses of bloom from winter to summer. Grow them in an indoor border or large pots of commercial mix, keep moist. Repot when necessary. Increase by cuttings late summer to autumn. *J. mesnyi* (*J. primulinum* primrose jasmine) evergreen rambler needing tying up to supports, flowers yellow, spring to summer. *J. polyanthum*, semi-evergreen twiner, fragrant pink-budded white flowers, winter to spring. Both grow to about 10ft(3m).

LAPAGERIA (Chilean bellflower)

An outstandingly beautifully flowered twiner, *L. rosea* is evergreen, to 10ft(3m) or more, and has waxy bells of flowers of crimson-pink or blush from midsummer to autumn. Grow in humus-rich soil in a border or large pots of well-draining peat-based mix, keep moist, not saturated. Repot spring. Increase by layering in spring or by slow to germinate seed also in spring.

LEDEBOURIA

A lovely bulbous plant, *L. socialis* (silver squill) is better known under its former name *Scilla violacea*. It has up to 5 leaves, 2-4in(5-10cm) long, green splashed and mottled silvery-green above, purple below, arising from above-ground purple bulbs which form large clumps. Small bell-shaped nodding flowers in loose spikes 4-5in(10-12.5cm) tall, white-margined green, stamens purple. Grow in pots of loam-based mix kept just moist – never saturated. Repot and increase by offsets in autumn.

177

LEPTOSPERMUM

Small-leaved, evergreen shrubs the branches of which may become smothered with flowers in summer. Grow in well-drained soil in an indoor border or large pots of loam-based mix. Increase by cuttings in early summer. *L. lanigerum* (*L. cunninghamii* woolly tea tree), to 12ft(4m) or more eventually, silvery-haired leaves, grey leaved in the form sold as *L. cunninhamii*, flowers white. *L. scoparium* (tea tree, manuka) to 10ft(3m) or more, aromatic leaves, flowers white, pink or red; it has several named varieties including 'Chapmanii' with brownish leaves and large rose flowers, 'Nanum' only 1ft(30cm) tall, rose flowers, 'Nichollsii' red-crimson flowers.

LILIUM (lily)

Many lilies make showy flowering pot plants and a number are deliciously scented too. Grow in pots of loam-based mix kept only just moist until the bulbs start to grow when they may be watered freely, keep ventilated and shaded in hot weather. Feed fortnightly when in flower. Pot autumn and increase by offsets then, by stem bulblets of some varieties which will take a few years to flower. Lilies may also be forced (treat as for hyacinths) and flower in about 3 months. *L. auratum* (golden-rayed lily) to 6ft(1.8m) or more, huge white gold-rayed flowers. *L. longiflorum eximium* (Easter lily) to 3ft(90cm) long, fragrant white flowers. *L. nepalense*, to 3ft(90cm), yellow to greenish, purple-suffused, fragrant flowers. *L. speciosum* (Japanese lily) to 5ft(1.5m) flowers wide, white spotted rose, fragrant. The above is a small selection of suitable species: there are many more hybrids to choose from too and among the best are the Mid-Century group which include: 'Cinnabar', maroon; 'Destiny', brown-spotted yellow; 'Enchantment', red; 'Harmony', orange.

MUTISIA (climbing gazania)

The large, beautifully coloured, daisy-like flowers distinguish these climbing evergreen shrubs. Grow in any commercial mix, keep moist and shade from strong sun. Repot and increase by seed in spring, cuttings in spring or late summer. *M. clematis*, to 10ft(3m) flowers orange scarlet, summer to autumn. *M. ilicifolia*, to 12ft(4m) or more, flowers rose to lilac. *M. oligodon*, 1½-4ft(45-120cm), flowers warm pink, is best grown climbing through a small shrub.

NARCISSUS (narcissus and daffodil) 22

A number of these familiar bulbous plants do well in pots if kept as cool as possible, especially at night when in flower to stop them withering. Grow in pots of any good mix and keep just moist. Pot bulbs as soon as possible, just covering the small types but leaving the necks of larger varieties a little above the surface, placing as many bulbs as will fill the pot with their sides almost touching. Keep outside buried under weathered ashes, peat or soil until shoots are about 2½in(6cm) long when they may be brought into a cool place indoors, in good light. When flowering is over plant outside. Increase by dividing clumps. Good varieties include, 'Double Event', double, white, orange centre; 'Dutch Master', trumpet, yellow; 'Fortune', yellow, large orange cup; 'Geranium', tazetta (bunch-flowered) types, white, orange red cups; 'Green Island', creamy, large yellow to green cup; 'Irene Copeland', double, yellow and white; 'La Riante', white, small rose-orange cup; 'Mount Hood', trumpet, cream; 'Paperwhite Grandiflora', tazetta cluster flowered, white; 'Snow Princess', white, small yellow cup edged orange.

PLEIONE

Free flowering dwarf orchids, about 6in(15cm) high, with comparatively large flowers. Grow in two parts of any commercial mix mixed with one part sphagnum moss, in pots or pans. Keep moist, shade from sun and ventilate well in summer. Feed fortnightly in summer. Repot after flowering in spring and increase by division then, leaving the top ⅔ of the pseudobulb above soil level. *P. bulbocodioides* (*P. formosana*, *P. limprichtii*, *P. pricei*), lilac to rosy mauve, lip pale blotched red, magenta or yellow, has several named varieties. *P. forrestii*, pale to deep yellow, lip blotched red. *P. praecox* (*P. lagenaria*, *P. wallichiana*), rose, lip creamy and pink.

POLYSTICHUM (shield fern)

Attractive ferns which are easy to grow. Grow in pots of any good mix, keep moist and shade from sun. Repot and increase by division in spring. *P. acrostichoides* (Christmas or dagger fern) evergreen fronds to 2ft(60cm), variable, some forms having crested or twisted leaflets. *P. aculeatum* (prickly shield fern) evergreen fronds glossy to 3ft(90cm). *P. lonchitis* (holly fern) evergreen leathery fronds to 2ft(60cm), leaflets spiny.

PUNICA 23

Long cultivated for its fruit, *P. granatum* (pomegranate) makes an excellent flowering and fruiting plant for large pots or tubs. Slow growing it may eventually reach 20ft(6m). The variety 'Nana', which flowers when quite small, grows to 6ft(1.8m). The crinkly petalled flowers are orange red and in the variety 'Flore Pleno' double, red, while 'Legrellei' has double, orange red flowers, streaked and margined white. Grow in loam-based mix. Keep well ventillated and watered in warm weather. Repot spring and increase by seed or layering then, or by cuttings in summer.

RHODODENDRON

A large genus of attractive flowering shrubs which includes the plants known as azaleas and many of which make excellent plants for large pots or tubs. Grow in special rhododendron mix or other peat-based acid mix. Keep moist but not overwatered and well ventilated spring to autumn. Shade from strong sun. Repot autumn or spring. Increase by seed in spring, sown on the surface; it will take some years to produce flowering plants, cuttings taken late summer to autumn may flower in their first year – this method is most suitable for small-leaved plants. Large-leaved plants may be increased by layering in spring. *R. edgeworthii*, including *R. bullatum*, evergreen, to about 4ft(1.2m) in pots, flowers fragrant, white variably flushed yellow, pink or both. *R. johnstoneanum*, evergreen, may slowly reach 6ft(1.8m) in pots, flowers fragrant, white to yellow with a yellow blotch, spotted red inside. *R. simsii*, semi-evergreen to evergreen, 3-6ft(90-180cm), flowers pink to deep red; a parent of many hybrids sold as Indian azaleas with flowers in many shades of pink, red, crimson and white, single or double.

SARRACENIA (pitcher plant) 24

Carnivorous plants with rosettes of leaves and attractive flowers. The leaves form cylinders which hold liquid and secrete a sugary bait attracting insects. Grow in pans of a half-and-half mix of peat and sphagnum moss topped with live sphagnum, or in just live sphagnum and stand in larger pans or trays of water. Keep moist and shaded from hot sun and a humid atmosphere. Increase by seed in spring in similarly filled pans. *S. flava* (yellow pitcher plant, trumpets) leaves yellowish green, purple throated or entirely purple, trumpet shaped, to 2ft(60cm) in pans, flowers 4in(10cm) across, yellow, nodding. *S. leucophylla* (*S. drummondii* lace trumpets) leaves green turning to white near the top, purple veined, trumpet shaped, to 3ft(90cm) in pans, flowers 4in(10cm) across, purple, nodding. *S. purpurea* (common pitcher plant) leaves green suffused and veined purple, reclining rather than fully upright to 1ft(30cm) long, flowers to 2½in(6.5cm) across, purple, nodding. A number of colourful hybrids are now also available.

SAXIFRAGA (saxifrage)

Excellent in hanging baskets or trailing down the sides of pots, *S. stolonifera* (mother-of-thousands, strawberry geranium) develops runners from which new plants arise in the manner of strawberry plants. The leaves are roundish, green above, purple to pink below, or in the variety 'Tricolor' (magic carpet saxifrage) shades of green and white suffused pink. Flowers small, whitish in loose spikes to 1½ft (45cm) tall. Grow in pots or baskets of loam-based mix. Repot spring. Increase by removing plantlets.

TORENIA (wishbone flower)

An annual plant with subtly attractive flowers, *T. fournieri* (bluewings) makes a bushy plant to 1ft(30cm) tall. The 4-lobed flowers are mainly pale purplish violet with 3 deep purplish-violet lobes and a yellow blotch in the central lower one, or in 'Alba', white with the yellow blotch, while 'Grandiflora' has larger flowers. Grow in any good potting mix. Shade from strong sun and feed fortnightly when in flower. Increase from seed in spring.

TULIPA (tulip)

Most tulips will do well as temporary pot plants, but best from bulbs purchased annually. Grow in pots of any good potting mix and keep just moist. Pot the bulbs in autumn placing them virtually side by side to fill the chosen size of pot, bury the pots outside under peat or weathered ashes. Leave until the shoots are 1-2in(2.5-5cm) high and bring indoors into a light position with a temperature of about 50°F(10°C) and then place in a bright but not sunny spot. If flowered in a warmer place by day put back into the cooler spot by night. The best varieties for indoor growing are the Single Early and Double Early types, which bloom at about 15in(38cm) tall. Single Earlies include 'Bellona' yellow, 'Brilliant Star' scarlet, 'Diana' white, 'Keizerskroon' yellow striped red, 'Pink Beauty' rose pink and white, 'Vander Neer' purple; Double Earlies include 'Electra' mauve pink, 'Maréchal Niel' yellow, 'Wilhelm Kordes' orange yellow flashed red, and 'Vuurbaak' scarlet.

List 4 Indoor water plants

The plants listed here are suitable for decorative purposes in indoor pools of differing temperature regimes.

ACORUS

An attractive marginal plant, *A. gramineus* (grassy-leaved sweet flag) forms tufts of green leaves, or in 'Variegatus' green, striped white, up to 1½ft(45cm) long. The flowers are insignificant. Grow in pots of loam-based mix always kept moist. Repot and increase by division in spring. For an unheated situation.

APONOGETON

The remarkable leaves of this plant are reduced to the veins giving *A. madagascariensis* (*A. fenestralis*), the popular names of latticeleaf or laceleaf. They are about 6in(15cm) long and submerged. Grow underwater in pots of loam-based mix in good light. Repot spring and increase by division then. The water temperature should be at 60°F(16°C) or more.

CYPERUS (galingale, umbrella sedge)

Splendid, rather grass-like plants suitable for shallow water or pots in water. Grow in pots of good loam-based mix and stand the pots in water. Repot spring and increase by division then. Temperature 54°F(12°C) or more. *C. alternifolius* (umbrella plant) stems clump forming, 1½-3ft(45-90cm) tall topped by a flower cluster from which radiate, as umbrella ribs, green leaf-like bracts up to 1ft(30cm) long. The leaves of variety 'Variegatus' are striped with white. *C. papyrus* (papyrus, paper plant) stems clump forming 4-10ft(1.2-3m) or more, dark green and topped by a mop-like flower cluster.

EICHHORNIA

A beautiful flowering plant, *E. crassipes* (water hyacinth) is a floating weed from tropical America. The plant floats by its bulbous leaf stalks, which are filled with airy spongy material. It does not need to be rooted but does best in a muddy-bottomed pool, or tank, with water at least 1ft(30cm) deep. Flowers in clusters, lavender. Plants may be transferred to grow outside during the summer but otherwise should be grown in a minimum temperature of 57°F(14°C). Increase by division of young plants in summer.

ELODEA (waterweed, pondweed)

The various species of waterweed are all rather similar, *E. canadensis* (Canadian waterweed) has trailing stems 20-40in(50-100cm) long and small leaves in groups of 3, rapidly growing and forming submerged mats; *E. crispa* (*Lagarosiphon muscoides, L. major*), similar but stems shorter and leaves in rings; *E. densa* (Brazilian waterweed) similar but larger and leaves in groups of 4-5. They are all excellent oxygenators. Grow in pools or tanks with a muddy bottom or in pots of loam-based mix or floating in nutrient-rich water, planting in spring. Thin out congested masses in autumn. Propagation is unlikely to be necessary but increase if required by division in spring. Suitable for most temperatures.

HYDROCHARIS

A floating plant, *H. morsus-ranae* (frog-bit) has submerged stems from which the tiny rounded lily-like leaves arise to the surface. The flowers are white and three petalled. In autumn the plant breaks up having formed resting buds which sink to the bottom for the winter. Increase, if necessary, by dividing stems with roots or resting buds. Hardy but tolerating a wide temperature range.

HYDROCLEYS
An attractively flowered floating plant, *H. nymphoides* (water poppy) is easy to grow in pools or tanks, or on its own in large containers filled ⅔ with loam-based mix and filled with water to the top. The stems root as they grow and produce spongy, roundish floating leaves and beautiful yellow poppy-like flowers in early summer. Increase by division. Fairly temperature tolerant.

NELUMBO (water lotus)
Beautifully flowered plants with large parasol-like leaves rising from the water on long stalks. Grow in large tubs, tanks or pools planting the roots in pots or water plant baskets of 1½ft(45cm) diameter or more, in a rich mix of half-and-half loam and rotted manure and covered with 6-12in(15-30cm) of water. Repot annually in spring and increase by division of the rhizomatous roots then or by seed. *N. lutea* (American lotus) leaves floating and rising on stems up to 7ft(2.1m) tall, blue green 1-2ft(30-60cm) across, flowers yellow, scented, up to 10in(25cm) across and on stems rising above the leaves. *N. nucifera* (sacred lotus) similar to *N. lutea* but leaves to 3ft(90cm) across and bluer green, flowers deep pink through to white, very fragrant. Extremely tolerant of a wide range of temperatures.

NYMPHAEA (water lily)   25
Superb flowering plants, the tropical water lilies may produce bloom through summer and autumn. They need large tanks or indoor pools. Grow in the soil at the bottom of the tank or pool or in baskets of soil made of ¾ loam-based mix, ¼ rotted manure with the addition of a little high phosphate fertilizer, all topped with gravel and planted so that the top of the crown just remains uncovered. Put in water to 1ft(30cm) above. Increase by root division or by plantlets formed by some varieties. Minimum temperature 70°F/21°C. The following is a small selection of hybrids, all are scented to some degree, they flower by day unless otherwise stated. 'B.C. Berry', crimson red, night; 'Director George T. Moore', violet blue; 'Emily Grant Hutchings', pinkish red, night; 'General Pershing', pink; 'Missouri', white, night; 'Mrs George H. Pring', white splashed crimson; and 'St Louis', yellow.

ORONTIUM
An unusual aquatic flowering arum, *O. aquaticum* (golden club) has an inconspicuous outer flower shell or spathe but a conspicuous, bright yellow centre spike or spadix, 4in(10cm) long, above water. The broad leaves, up to 1ft(30cm) long form tufts and float in deep water. Grow in pools or tanks of water about 1ft(30cm) deep, in pots or baskets of half-and-half loam-based mix and rotted manure. Increase by division in spring. Fairly temperature tolerant.

PISTIA
A floating plant forming rosettes of leaves and developing into large colonies, *P. stratiotes* (water lettuce) has pale green, roundish leaves. Float on shallow water preferably over a muddy bottom, shade in summer from strong sun. Increase by division in summer. Water temperature about 70°F(21°C).

PONTEDERIA   26
The glossy green, heart-shaped leaves and spikes of densely packed blue flowers make *P. cordata* (pickerel weed) an attractive water plant. It grows 2-4ft(60-120cm). Grow in less than 1ft(30cm) of water in containers of half and half loam-based mix and decayed manure or in the muddy pool bottom. Increase by division in spring. Tolerant of most temperatures.

SALVINIA
Floating foliage plants with rather fern-like leaves on the water but hair-like ones below, and forming colonies on water at about 65°F(18°C). Increase by division. *S. auriculata*, curved, boat-shaped leaves to 1in(2.5cm) long and 1¾in(4.5cm) wide, on plants to 10in(25cm) long. *S. rotundifolia* (floating moss) roundish floating leaves ⅝in(16mm) long by ¾in(19mm) wide, on plants up to 2¾in(7cm) long.

181

List 5 Outdoor plants
These are hardy subjects for planting outside conservatories and garden rooms to provide screens and decorative effect when viewed from within or from the outside.

CHAENOMELES (flowering quince) 27
Lovely flowering shrubs for decorating the walls outside and around garden rooms and which are easily kept in shape by pruning. They will grow in nearly all soils, plant late autumn to spring. Increase by cuttings or layering in late summer. The fruit may be used for preserves. *C. speciosa* (Japanese quince) shrubby, about 6ft(1.8m), flowers red, white or pink to crimson according to variety. *C. × superba*, shrubby, about 6ft(1.8m), flowers orange red, white or pink to crimson according to variety.

CHIMONANTHUS
Superbly scented flowers in winter to fill the air outside a garden room, appear before the leaves on the shrub *C. praecox* (*C. fragrans* wintersweet). The flowers are pale yellow with a purplish centre on a shrub up to 10ft(3m) tall and suitable for growing against a wall. Grows in most soils but add humusy, moisture-retentive material to light ones. Plant late autumn to spring. Prune after flowering to keep in shape. Increase by layering in autumn.

CHOISYA (Mexican orange blossom)
C. ternata is a fine evergreen shrub which is not absolutely hardy but maybe grown against a wall for protection, the scented white flowers appear in spring. Grow in well-draining soil and plant in autumn or late spring. Should only need little pruning to keep in shape, slow growing but up to 10ft(3m) high. Increase by cuttings in late summer.

CLEMATIS 28
Marvellously flowered climbing plants to decorate outside walls or provide shade in summer. Grow in well dug, rich, moisture-retentive soil which does not get too hot in summer, if planting in a sunny site use another plant to provide shade for the roots. Plant from late autumn to spring. Prune if necessary to keep growth in check after flowering, or for those varieties which flower twice after the first flowering.

Late flowers may be pruned more severely in spring. Increase by cuttings in midsummer. There is a great range of large-flowered climbers which may be chosen to cover a wall or other structure according to colour, the species and their varieties described below are generally much more graceful plants and may be used for specific purposes. *C. alpina*, a super little climber which may be left to tumble down steps leading from a door, 4-6ft(1.2-1.8m), flowers blue but with bright blue, pink and white varieties. *C. macropetala*, 6-10ft(1.8-3m), suitable for growing up window or door sides, nodding flowers of violet blue, with lavender, pink and white varieties. *C. montana*, a massive climber suitable for screening and shading, to 25ft(7.6m) or more, flowers white turning pink, fragrant and with deep to light pink and white varieties. *C. orientalis*, a massive climber to 20ft(6m) or more, suitable for screening and overhanging so that its nodding yellow flowers may be looked up into; a long flowering season from June to November, the later flowers mingling with the silver seed heads of the earlier flowers; the petals are thick in the usually cultivated form.

DRIMYS 29
A double value evergreen shrub or tree, *D. winteri* (winter's bark) has aromatic foliage, usually rather broadly willow-like but variable, and scented creamy flowers in early summer. Not fully hardy it needs a sheltered site, such as the corner angle that might be provided between a garden room extension and the house and where it could provide a permanent screen with its silvery undersided light green leaves. Capable of reaching 50ft(15m) as a tree it is more likely to be grown as a large bush. Grow in moisture-retentive but well-draining soil. Plant in spring. Increase by cuttings in summer.

ECCREMOCARPUS (glory flower)
A climbing evergreen, scrambling up and over objects by means of leaf tendrils, *E. scaber* (Chilean

25 *Nymphaea* var (water lily)
27 *Chaenomeles speciosa* var (Japanese quince)
29 *Drimys winteri* var (winter's bark)

26 *Pontederia cordata* (pickerel weed)
28 *Clematis macropetala*
30 *Parthenocissus tricuspidata* var (Boston ivy, Japanese creeper)

glory flower) has tubular flowers of brilliant orange – lighter towards the open end, or in some forms yellow or red, in large clusters, from late spring to autumn. It may grow to 20ft(6m) but unfortunately is not fully hardy and often cut down unless in a very sheltered position where it could provide a good screen. Easily raised from seed it may be grown as an annual screen in cooler sites. Sow in early spring and after hardening off plant out in early summer; it will grow in most soils but does need something for its tendrils to grip and in fact will grow well with a darker leaved ivy, for instance.

LAURUS (sweet bay)
An amenable evergreen shrub which can grow 15ft(4.5m) but may be clipped or pruned to fill its allotted space L. *nobilis* (bay) may be used as a screen to hide low walls supporting garden rooms, to provide columns at door sides or steps leading to a garden room or conservatory, or be grown in tubs or other suitably large containers at the head of such a flight of steps. The leaves are widely used in cooking. Grow in any good soil or potting mix, in sun or partial shade, and plant in spring. Increase by cuttings in late summer or by detaching suckers.

LAVANDULA (lavender)
Attractively flowered and foliaged evergreen shrubs with aromatic leaves and stems. Excellent where a low screen is required, such as below a garden room window or to provide root shade for clematis. Grow in free-draining soil in sun, and plant in spring. Increase by late summer cuttings. L. *angustifolia* (L. *officinalis*, L. *spica*, L. *vera* English lavender) 2-3ft(60-90cm) sometimes more, lilac-violet flowers or, according to variety, violet, pink or white. L. *stoechas* (French lavender) 1-3ft(30-90cm), violet flowers topped by a leafy violet tuft.

MAHONIA
Excellent evergreen shrubs with delightful, often strongly scented, clusters or long drooping tails or upright spikes of yellow flowers. Superb low screening plants very suitable for providing shade for the roots of tall climbing clematis or hiding a low wall such as that supporting some conservatories. They will grow in most soils but prefer those rich in

humus, and in sun or shade. Plant in spring or autumn. Increase by detaching suckers if available in spring or cuttings in summer. M. *aquifolium* (Oregon grape) 4-6ft(1.2-1.8m) but easily pruned down to any required height, flowers in thick clusters through spring, strongly scented, followed by decorative blue-black berries. M. *bealei*, 6-7ft(1.8-2.1m), flowers in short erect spikes, late winter to spring. M. *japonica*, 6-7ft(1.8-2.1m), flowers in drooping spikes, strongly scented, winter to spring.

PARTHENOCISSUS 30
The two deciduous climbers described are both excellent for covering walls, even roofs if allowed, the leaves turning to brilliant colours in autumn. Suitable for covering such structures as extensions or arbors. Grow in any reasonably fertile soil in sun or semi-shade. Increase by cuttings in autumn. P. *quinquefolia* (Virginia creeper) 60-70ft(18-21m), leaves hand like with 5 leaflets which turn red to crimson. P. *tricuspidata* (Boston ivy, Japanese creeper) 60-70ft(18-21m), leaves usually 3-lobed and turning scarlet to crimson in the autumn.

ROSMARINUS (rosemary)
A fine evergreen shrub with strongly aromatic foliage, useful in the kitchen, R. *officinalis*, is an upright or straggling bush with bright lavender blue to pale lavender, or white flowers. The leaves have a deep green upper surface but are silvery below, densely packed. Excellent for screen or against low walls, or to provide shelter or shade, 2-4ft(60-120cm), or more, tall. Grow in free-draining soil in a warm, sunny site, and plant spring or autumn. Increase by cuttings in late summer or autumn.

SANTOLINA
Fine foliaged yellow-flowered, evergreen shrubby plants which are low growing and suitable as living skirting boards for the outside walls of conservatories and other garden rooms. Grow in free-draining soil in a sunny position, and plant in spring or autumn. Increase by cuttings in late summer or autumn. S. *chamaecyparissus* (S. *incana* lavender cotton) to 2ft(60cm), leaves silvery, flowers buff yellow. S. *virens* (S. *viridis*), to 2ft(60cm), leaves bright green, flowers bright yellow.

TROPAEOLUM (nasturtium)

The two climbers described here have attractive flowers and foliage and are both suitable for training beside door frames or windows, the Canary creeper is also excellent grown in urns or tubs. Grow in good moisture-retentive but free-draining soil. Increase the Canary creeper by seed in spring, the flame flower by seed or division in spring. *T. peregrinum* (Canary creeper), a short-lived perennial grown as an annual, to 15ft(4.5m) leaves light green, usually 5-lobed, flowers brilliant yellow with curiously shaped fringed petals. *T. speciosum* (flame flower) a perennial growing from fleshy, rhizomatous roots, to 12ft(3.7m) green 6-lobed leaves, flowers nasturtium-like, vivid scarlet-red.

VITIS (grape)

All the grapes described here have beautiful foliage, sometimes really glorious in the autumn. They climb vigorously by means of tendrils and need some form of support for these to twine around, such as a pergola sheltering a garden room door or on trellis panels against a wall. Grow in free-draining, humus-rich soil, in full or partial sun. Increase by cuttings in autumn. *V.* × 'Brant' (*V. vinifera* 'Brandt'), to 30ft(9m) or more, leaves deep green turning brilliant shades of orange and red to crimson in autumn; will produce edible grapes in favourable conditions. *V. coignetiae* (crimson glory vine) to 90ft(27m) suitable for large structures, has huge, roundish to slightly lobed leaves which turn bright orange, red and crimson in autumn. *V. vinifera* 'Purpurea' (Teinturier grape) usually restricted 10ft(3m) or more, young leaves claret-red turning purple.

WISTERIA

Magnificent where they may be trained so that the long hanging clusters of flowers may be seen to advantage, such as against a wall, over an archway or entrance. Grow in rich but free-draining soil in sun, and plant spring or autumn. Increase by layering in spring or cuttings in summer. *W. floribunda* (Japanese wisteria) to 35ft(10m) or more, leaves with 13-19 leaflets, flowers lavender to purple in long drooping clusters, in 'Macrobotrys' (*W. multijuga*), up to 3ft(90cm) long, and in 'Alba' the flowers are white. *W. sinensis* (Chinese wisteria) much like the preceding but leaves usually with 11 leaflets and flowers appearing before the leaves, lavender, purple or white in drooping clusters to 1ft(30cm) long.

Picture Credits & Acknowledgments

2 National Monuments Record
6 National Monuments Record © C.L.S. Cornwall-Legh
9 Michael Dunne/EWA; Design: Earl Burn Combs
12 Amdega Limited
13 Spike Powell/EWA; Owner: David and Babs King
14 Camera Press/Schoner Wohnen
17 Michael Crockett/EWA; Design: Nicholas Haslam
19 J.A. Nearing Co., Inc.
20-22 Peter Bailey/The World of Interiors
24 Michael Boys/Susan Griggs Agency
27 Jerry Harpur
29 Neil Lorimer/EWA
31 Ian Yeomans/Susan Griggs Agency
33 English Greenhouse Products Corporation, USA
34 Camera Press/Austral
36 top Groen, *Den Nederlandtsen Hovenier*, 1670
36 centre G. Sinclair, *Hortus Ericaeus Woburnensis*, 1825
36 bottom Mary Evans Picture Library
37 top Pierre Boitard, *Traité de la Composition et de l'Ornement des Jardins*, 3rd edition 1825
37 bottom *Gardeners' Chronicle*, 1891
38 Mary Evans Picture Library
39 top Franz Antoine, *Der Wintergarten in der Kaiserlichen Königlichen Hofburg zu Wien*, 1852
39 bottom & 40 Mary Evans Picture Library
41 top From a postcard in the collection of Dr B. Elliott
41 bottom From a catalogue issued by W. Richardson and Co., *c.* 1910
41 Michael Dunne
43 Michael Nicholson/EWA; Design: Dorit Egli
45 Tim Street-Porter/EWA
46 Michael Nicholson/EWA; Design: Ken Turner
47 Jerry Tubby/EWA
49 Michael Dunne/EWA; Design: Muller & Murphy

50 Mike Burgess
53 Michael Boys/Susan Griggs Agency
55 Michael Nicholson/EWA; Design: Blind Alley
74 both Andersen Corporation, Bayport, MN
77 Michael Crockett/EWA
79 Michael Nicholson/EWA; Design: Virginia Brier
80 Linda Burgess
83 Camera Press/Zuhause
84 Good Housekeeping/Jan Baldwin
88 Camera Press Ltd/Schöner Wohnen
89 from *Rustic Adornments*, Shirley Hibberd, London, 1895
91 Richard Bryant/Arcaid
93 English Greenhouse Products Corporation, USA
94 Machin Designs Limited
101 Linda Burgess
104 National Monuments Record
107 left Crittall Warmlife Limited
107 right BACO Leisure Products Limited
109 both Dolan/Macrae Associates
111 Michael Boys/Susan Griggs Agency
118 English Greenhouse Products Corporation, USA
121 Neil Lorimer/EWA
122 Sun System Solar Greenhouses
123 Tim Street-Porter/EWA
125 Linda Burgess
127 Michael Boys/Susan Griggs Agency
129 Neil Lorimer/EWA
131 Tim Street-Porter/EWA; Design: Michael Hopkins
133 Linda Burgess
135 Neil Lorimer/EWA
137 Machin Designs Limited
138 Michael Boys/Susan Griggs Agency
140 from *Rustic Adornments*, Shirley Hibberd, 3rd edition, 1870
141 Michael Dunne/EWA; Owner: Laura Ponti
143 Michael Dunne/EWA
144 Pamla Toler/Impact Photos
153-183 Rainbird

The editors would like to thank the following companies for their assistance:

Aluminium Greenhouses Inc., USA; Amdega Limited; Andersen Corporation, Bayport, MN; Aston Home Extensions; Alexander Bartholomew Conservatories Limited; BACO Leisure Products Limited; Chelsea Physic Garden; Crittall Warmlife Limited; Crusader Conservatories; Eden Conservatories; Geoge H. Elt Limited; English Greenhouse Products Corporation, USA; Essential Structures Research Associates (ESRA) Limited; David Fennings (Professional Conservatory Specialists); Frost & Co.; Grosvenor Products Limited; LECS Housing; The Lindley Library, Royal Horticultural Society; Machin Designs Limited; The Metallic Constructions Co., (Derby), Limited; J.A. Nearing Co., Inc.; Parwin Power Heaters; Shilton Garden Services Limited; Sun System Solar Greenhouses.

Index

Index of Plants